# MICHAEL EATON

**BOOKS**

**WORD BOOKS**
Nelson Word Ltd
Milton Keynes, England
WORD AUSTRALIA
Kilsyth, Victoria, Australia
WORD COMMUNICATIONS LTD
Vancouver, B.C., Canada
STRUIK CHRISTIAN BOOKS (PTY) LTD
Cape Town, South Africa
CHRISTIAN MARKETING NEW ZEALAND LTD
Havelock North, New Zealand
JENSCO LTD
Hong Kong
JOINT DISTRIBUTORS SINGAPORE –
ALBY COMMERCIAL ENTERPRISES PTE LTD
and
CAMPUS CRUSADE, ASIA LTD
SALVATION BOOK CENTRE
Malaysia

ISBN 0-85009-607-6 (Australia 1-86258-289-0)

Unless otherwise indicated, Scripture quotations are from the New International Version (NIV), © 1973, 1978, 1984 by International Bible Society.
Other Scripture quotations are from the following sources:
The New American Standard Bible (NASB), © 1960, 1962, 1963, 1968, 1971, 1972, 1973, 1975, 1977 the Lockman Foundation.
The Authorised Version of the Bible (AV).


The quotations in the following studies are all used by permission.
**Study 3** from *The Grandeur of God*, by C. Samuel Storms, © 1984. Baker Book House, Grand Rapids, Michigan.
**Study 4** from *Restoration in the Church*, by Terry Virgo, © Terry Virgo 1985. Kingsway Publications, Lottbridge Drove, Eastbourne, East Sussex, BN23 6NL.
**Studies 5, 27** from *The Practice of Godliness*, by Jerry Bridges, © 1983 by Jerry Bridges. NavPress.
**Study 6** from *The Grace Awakening*, by Charles R. Swindoll, © 1990 by Charles R. Swindoll. Nelson Word Ltd.
**Study 7** from *The Best of A.W. Tozer*, compiled by Warren Wiersbe, © 1978. Baker Book House, USA. Crossway Books.
**Studies 8, 24** from *Prayers of Life*, by Michel Quoist, © Les Editions Ouvrières, Paris 1954. Gill and Macmillan Ltd/North America, Sheed & Ward, Kansas City.
**Study 9** from *The Normal Christian Life*, by Watchman Nee, © 1961 Angus I. Kinnear. Kingsway Publications.
**Study 9** from *Sanctified Through the Truth*, by D. Martyn Lloyd-Jones, Copyright © Bethan Lloyd-Jones 1989. Kingsway Publications Ltd.
**Study 10** from *The Pursuit of Holiness*, by Jerry Bridges, © 1978. NavPress.
**Study 11** from *Straightforward*, by Larry Tomczak, © 1978. Bridge Publishing Inc.
**Study 12** from *Knowing God*, by J.I. Packer, © 1973. Hodder & Stoughton Ltd.
**Study 13** from *Hope and Suffering*, by Rt. Revd. Desmond Tutu, © D.M. Tutu, 1983. Skotaville.
**Study 14** from *Inside Out*, by Dr. Larry Crabb, © 1988 by Larry Crabb. NavPress.
**Study 15** from *The Presence of the Future*, by G.E. Ladd, © 1974 by George Eldon Ladd. SPCK.
**Studies 16, 17** from *A Gardener Looks at the Fruits of the Spirit*, by W. Phillip Keller, © W. Phillip Keller 1979. Nelson Word Ltd.
**Study 18** from *Life in Christ*, by John Stott, Text copyright © 1979, 1991 John Stott. Kingsway Publications Ltd.
**Studies 19, 21** from *Galatians & Ephesians*, by William Hendriksen, © 1968 by William Hendriksen. The Banner of Truth Trust.
**Study 20** from *Songs of My Soul*, by W. Phillip Keller, © 1989 by W. Phillip Keller. Nelson Word Ltd.
**Study 22** from *Learning to Love People You Don't Like*, by Floyd McClung, © Floyd McClung Jr 1987. Kingsway Publications Ltd.
**Study 23** from *How to Live the Christian Life*, by Selwyn Hughes, © Selwyn Hughes 1974, 1981. Kingsway Publications/USA and Philippines, Edward England.
**Studis 26, 30** from *The Heart of the Gospel*, by Martyn Lloyd-Jones, © Bethan Lloyd-Jones. Crossway Books.
**Study 29** from *Spiritual Depression*, by Martyn Lloyd-Jones, © 1965 D. Martyn Lloyd-Jones. Published by Marshall Pickering an imprint of HarperCollins Publishers Ltd.


*Created, designed and typeset by* Frontier Publishing International Ltd., BN43 6RE, England. *Reproduced, printed and bound in Great Britain for* Nelson Word Ltd. *by* Bushey Mead Press.

93 94 95 96 / 10 9 8 7 6 5 4 3 2 1

# Making the most of the studies ...

Welcome to the Oasis study entitled *Walk by the Spirit!* God wants us to know what it means to live not by rules, but in response to His voice. This book encourages us to abandon a legalistic relationship with Him and to develop a lifestyle consistent with the Gospel.

We suggest that you take two days to cover each study and therefore two months to complete the book. You might want to work through the material more quickly, but if you take your time you are likely to benefit more. We recommend that you use the New International Version of the Bible (post-1983 version). The important thing is not that you finish fast, but that you hear from God *en route!* So aim to learn well and steadily build the teaching into your life.

When Jesus fulfilled the law for us, He released us from the need to live by rules and opened up a relationship with Himself. We 'serve in the new way of the Spirit, and not in the old way of the written code' (Rom. 7:6b).

Michael Eaton helps us to understand how we can enjoy the freedom that Christ came to give us. He tells us how we can 'inherit the kingdom' by putting to death the deeds of the flesh and by cultivating the fruit of the Spirit. He also teaches on subjects such as overcoming temptation; restoring someone who has sinned; sowing and reaping; avoiding weariness and boasting only in the cross of Christ.

The three sections under the main text relate to the teaching material. You may be asked to consider some aspect of the Christian life, to write down an answer, or to do something practical. The questions have been designed to help you to escape from legalism and to enjoy a deeper intimacy with the Holy Spirit. Let the Scripture verses inspire you in your walk with God.

The Bible says, 'Wise men store up knowledge' (Prov. 10:14), and Jesus underlines this when He calls us to '[bring] good things out of the good stored up in [our] heart' (Luke 6:45).

God wants to encourage and inform you through His Word. That's what the 'Food for thought' section is all about. It gives you the invaluable opportunity to hear direct from God and to store up what He says to you. **Please use a separate notebook** particularly for this section. Not only will it help you to crystallise your thoughts, but it will also be of tremendous reference value in the future.

As you study, refuse to let time pressurise you. Pray that God will speak to you personally and expect Him to do so. You may sometimes find that you're so enthralled by what He says to you that you're looking up many Scriptures which are not even suggested!

Finally, may God bless you as you work through this book. May He help you to guard against legalism and enjoy the freedom of His Spirit.

# A yoke of slavery

The son by the bondwoman was born according to the flesh, and the son by the free woman through the promise ... 'CAST OUT THE BONDWOMAN AND HER SON, FOR THE SON OF THE BONDWOMAN SHALL NOT BE AN HEIR WITH THE SON OF THE FREE WOMAN' ... It was for freedom that Christ set us free; therefore keep standing firm and do not be subject again to a yoke of slavery (Gal. 4:23,30b; 5:1 NASB).

The Galatians were floundering. They had received the good news about Jesus and had put their faith in Him. But after a while, certain people had come in and had tried to persuade them that they had to supplement the gospel of grace with the Law of Moses.

'This fellow Paul isn't paying sufficient attention to the commandments,' they were saying. 'Now that you've become Christians, you must get back to the moral law and submit to Jewish ceremonies. You've got to be circumcised and become an Israelite — only then will God accept you.'

When Paul discovered what was happening in the Galatian church, he was horrified and wrote a strong letter to the believers there. 'What are you doing?' he said. 'Don't you see that you can't mix the two covenants? Christ has released you from the Mosaic law, so why are you trying to put yourselves in bondage to it again? Law has no place alongside grace. You must abandon legalism because if you don't, it will ensnare you.'

The law is a 'yoke of slavery'. You can recognise people who wear it by their way of life. It's legalistic. 'I'm going to try to live up to

## ▓ To review

Review your relationship with the Lord.

Are you still enjoying it or has something changed? Think about any changes for good or bad; what was it that caused them?

## ▓ To meditate on

Christians are not under law.
'You are not under law, but under grace' (Rom. 6:14b).
'We have been released from the law so that we serve in the new way of the Spirit, and not in the old way of the written code' (Rom. 7:6b).
'Through the law I died to the law so that I might live for God' (Gal. 2:19).
'(Christ abolished) in his flesh the law with its commandments and regulations' (Eph. 2:15).

God's standards,' they say. 'So I'll keep the Ten Commandments and I'll do this and that. Then God will be pleased with me and accept me.'

Maybe your Christianity is legalistic. There was once a time when you knew such liberty. Jesus was wonderful and you really enjoyed your relationship with Him. But then things changed. Somehow you were persuaded that you had to obey certain 'laws' to please God. 'I've got to pray, read the Bible, give my tithe, go to church ...' you thought. And slowly, you lost your joy and became enslaved by the very faith that was supposed to set you free.

If you didn't achieve your goals, you'd feel guilty. Then you wouldn't be able to pray. The devil would whisper in your heart, 'What about this sin, and that?' And you'd feel that your Christian life was a total failure because you could never seem to live up to the standards that you felt that God was setting you.

What happened? You did exactly what the Galatians were doing — striving to obey the law in order to please God. That 'yoke of slavery' bends many people over and cripples their Christian life. They need to be set free to enjoy again the glorious liberty of the sons of God.

### ▓ To memorise

'But now, by dying to what once bound us, we have been released from the law so that we serve in the new way of the Spirit, and not in the old way of the written code' (Rom. 7:6).

➤ As a background to these studies, read through Galatians 1—4.

➤ Write down in a note book any verses which indicate how strongly Paul felt about what was happening in the Galatian church.

The law and the gospel cannot coexist. The law must disappear before the gospel. It is scarcely possible to estimate the strength of conviction and depth of prophetic insight which this declaration implies. The apostle thus confidently sounds the death-knell of Judaism at a time when one half of Christendom clung to the Mosaic law with a jealous affection little short of frenzy.
*Bishop Lightfoot*
*Word Studies in the New Testament*

# Stand firm

It was for freedom that Christ set us free; therefore keep standing firm and do not be subject again to a yoke of slavery (Gal. 5:1 NASB).

When Paul tells us that Christ has set us free, he's saying that Jesus has done for us what we could never do for ourselves. He knew that we were incapable of keeping the law, so He kept it for us. God declared that the soul that sinned would die (Ezek. 18:4). Jesus became sin for us and took the penalty of the law on Himself. When He died, He set us free from the law and opened another door to us — it's called grace.

Christianity has nothing to do with trying to live up to God's standards. It's about believing that Jesus has already met them. When we're saved, we no longer cower before God and whimper, 'I'm trying to do my best, Lord. I'm sorry I'm such a miserable failure.' We come to Him with confidence — not because we're looking at our performance, but because we're looking at Christ's.

Jesus has fully satisfied the Father on our behalf. When God looks at us, He sees Jesus' righteousness and accepts us totally. Our apparent failures will make no difference to our standing before God. He loves us not because of what we do, but because we're in His Son. He had no condemnation for Jesus, so He will

## ▓ To do

Keep a notebook with you for a whole day. Whenever you think or say 'I ought to,' 'I should,' or 'I must,' note it down.

At the end of the day assess the statements you have made and use this as an indicator as to whether or not you are standing firm.

## ▓ To meditate on

We can approach God boldly.
'In him and through faith in him we may approach God with freedom and confidence' (Eph. 3:12).
'Let us then approach the throne of grace with confidence, so that we may receive mercy and find grace to help us in our time of need' (Heb. 4:16).
'We have confidence to enter the Most Holy Place by the blood of Jesus ... let us draw near to God ... in full assurance of faith' (Heb. 10:19b,22a).

never condemn us. That's why we can always approach Him boldly. Access is not by law, but by grace.

'But,' you say, 'what if I stand before God and remember my sins?' Well, does the Bible say, 'If anyone sins, he comes under the judgement of the law?' No. It tells us that Jesus Christ is our advocate with the Father and that God will forgive us our sins if we confess them to Him (1 John 1:9). The focus of grace is not on judgement, but on mercy. Judgement fell on Jesus; mercy now comes to us.

Once we know that we're totally accepted by God, we will experience freedom. Now Paul warns us that we must stand firm in this freedom because we will be tempted to return to legalism. In other words, we'll try to add personal righteousness to the finished work of the Cross and will end up enslaved to rules and regulations.

So let me ask you, are you absolutely sure that God accepts you? Or are you somehow trying to earn your way into His presence? Christ has set you free. Live in that freedom and refuse to let anyone rob you of your complete security in Him.

➢ Read Matthew 5:17; Acts 13:39; Romans 8:2; 10:4; Hebrews 10:5–10.

➢ What do these Scriptures teach us about Jesus and the Law?

➢ What does this mean for us?

### ▓ To pray

Visualise someone walking straight up to the King or Queen, leaning on their throne and chatting to them. List qualities which such a relationship would have, e.g. familiarity, acceptance.

Now spend some time alone with the Lord, imagine yourself in that throne-room and enjoy your relationship with Him. Thank God for His wonderful grace. Remember that with this kind of relationship it is inappropriate to couch your thanks in religious phrases — just tell the Lord what you feel.

He delighteth in mercy, and will cast all your sins in the depths of the sea — that mystical, spiritual, wonderful sea, the sea of the grace of God.
*Alexander Whyte*
*The Expositors Dictionary of Texts*

# Severed from Christ

Behold I, Paul, say to you that if you receive circumcision, Christ will be of no benefit to you. And I testify again to every man who receives circumcision, that he is under obligation to keep the whole Law. You have been severed from Christ, you who are seeking to be justified by law; you have fallen from grace (Gal. 5:2-4 NASB).

The false teachers in Galatia were focusing on one area — circumcision. They wanted the believers to return to the Mosaic Law, and circumcision would be the sign that this was happening. Paul had to address the issue.

Now these Galatians were very sincere people. They really wanted to please God and the idea of supplementing grace with law appealed to them. So when Paul said, 'You've been severed from Christ and have fallen from grace' he wasn't declaring, 'You've obviously slipped into sin, so you've lost your salvation.' He was warning them, 'If you try to live your Christian life in a legalistic way, you will cut yourself off from the grace of Christ.'

False teachers are around today. 'You're not really a full Christian through faith in Christ,' they say. 'To be fully saved, you must live up to certain standards and feel that you're doing well. Then God will justify you.'

It's so easy to fall for this teaching because it sounds so logical. 'Christ has saved me,' we think. 'Now He expects me to work hard at my salvation.' So we submit to externally imposed rules and think, 'God is pleased if I spend two hours praying, but frowns if I manage only two

## ▓ To question

How is the term 'fallen from grace' used today?

_____

What is the real meaning of the phrase?

_____

## ▓ To meditate on

The law can't justify us.
'Has not Moses given you the law? Yet not one of you keeps the law' (John 7:19a).
'No-one will be declared righteous in his sight by observing the law; rather, through the law we become conscious of sin' (Rom. 3:20b).
'Know that a man is not justified by observing the law, but by faith in Jesus Christ' (Gal. 2:16a).

minutes.' Christianity becomes a battle to keep God happy. And we steadily lose our joy as we strive to attain impossible standards.

That's what it feels like to be 'severed from Christ'. Jesus hasn't abandoned us or pushed us out of the Kingdom. We've simply taken our eyes off Him. We've been attempting to justify ourselves when Jesus has already justified us. We've been trying to add works to His perfect sacrifice on the Cross. We've 'fallen from grace'. We've lost our sense of fellowship with God and no longer experience His joy and power.

Paul told the Galatians, 'If you submit to circumcision, you'll have to be consistent and keep the whole law.' He knew that the law would bless them only if they could follow it faultlessly, but since no one could do that, it was foolish to return to an impossible system.

The difference between being under law and grace is this: the law threatens punishment and condemns. Grace offers forgiveness and salvation. Law binds us to external rules; grace sets us free to serve Jesus through the indwelling Spirit. There's only one way to fulfil the Old Testament Law — you put your faith in Jesus and live solely for Him.

## ▨ To list

In a notebook make a list of external rules which people impose on themselves as means of pleasing God, e.g. I will go to church twice every Sunday.

Consider whether or not you are still living by rules. If you are, how do you think you can change this?

➢ Read Matthew 5:19; 15:9; 1 Timothy 1:3,4; 4:2; 6:3–5; 2 Timothy 4:3; Titus 1:10,11; 2 Peter 2:1.

➢ What are the characteristics of false teachers?

➢ In retrospect do you feel that anyone has ever given you any false teaching?

➢ Pray for your church; ask the Lord to protect it from false teaching and to anoint the preaching of *His* word.

**Grace ceases to be grace if God is compelled to bestow it in the presence of human merit.... Grace ceases to be grace if God is compelled to withdraw it in the presence of human demerit.... (Grace) is treating a person without the slightest reference to desert whatsoever, but solely according to the infinite goodness and sovereign purpose of God.**
*C. Samuel Storms*

# The law points to Christ

For we through the Spirit, by faith, are waiting for the hope of righteousness. For in Christ Jesus neither circumcision nor uncircumcision means anything (Gal. 5:5,6a NASB).

W e cannot begin to live for God until we've died to the law (Gal. 2:19). We can't live a holy life until we've escaped condemnation and have received God's full acceptance. Godliness begins with faith in Christ.

When Paul says that we're 'waiting for the hope of righteousness' he doesn't mean that we sit down and passively expect righteousness to happen. On the one hand we recognise that we are already righteous in Christ, while on the other, we seek to work out that righteousness in our lives through the Holy Spirit.

There's a 'hope of righteousness' for every believer. As we live out Christ's righteousness, He assures us that our work will be rewarded. The love that we extend to others 'through the Spirit, by faith' will not remain unnoticed. We have a certain hope that one day Jesus will say to us, 'Well done, good and faithful servant.'

Where faith is paramount, circumcision is irrelevant. Now circumcision may not be a typical modern-day problem, but we can still mistakenly put ourselves under something that is characteristic of the Mosaic covenant.

The heart of that covenant lay in the legal and sacrificial system. The first person to be

## ▓ To consider

How should we work out righteousness in our lives?

_____

_____

_____

## ▓ To meditate on

Christ has superseded the law.
'Through him everyone who believes is justified from everything you could not be justified from by the law of Moses' (Acts 13:39).
'Christ is the end of the law' (Rom. 10:4a).
'The former regulation is set aside because it was weak and useless (for the law made nothing perfect), and a better hope is introduced, by which we draw near to God' (Heb. 7:18,19).

circumcised was Abraham. Circumcision symbolised that he was justified by faith and pointed to the coming Messiah who would justify people in the same way. When Moses introduced the law, the entire system — sacrifices, ceremonies, tabernacle, etc. — looked forward to an ultimate fulfilment in Christ.

Since Christ has now fulfilled the law, the Mosaic system has become redundant. The writer to the Hebrews tells us that the blood of bulls and goats could never take away sins (Heb. 10:4). In itself, the old sacrificial system did nothing more than point to Jesus. 'So,' says Paul, 'there's no value in circumcision. It won't bless you or anyone else. Its function was merely to direct attention to Jesus.'

Modern-day circumcision is seen in people who trust in baptism, confirmation, church-going, praying, etc. But their religious lifestyle means nothing. Uncircumcision is seen in people who don't do religious things but still think they're OK with God. Their irreligious lifestyle does nothing for them either. It's no good being proud of your sort of circumcision or uncircumcision. Both are irrelevant under the new covenant which points to Christ.

> ➤ Read Hebrews 7—10.
>
> ➤ In your own words summarise the content of each chapter in a notebook.

### ▓ To discover

How does Paul define New Testament circumcision? (See Rom. 2:29; Col. 2:11,12.)

_____

_____

_____

**Nothing has hindered the growth of the kingdom more than the ugly face of legalism. The devil realizes that undermining the very character of the gospel is far more effective than opposing it blatantly because he then reduces it to the level of an irrelevant religion.**
*Terry Virgo*

# Faith working through love

For in Christ Jesus neither circumcision nor uncircumcision means anything, but faith working through love (Gal. 5:6 NASB).

Jesus, who was born under the law, is the only one who has ever kept it. He was circumcised, He worshipped at the synagogue and fulfilled every requirement of God in the Scriptures. He was obedient even to the Cross where He took the punishment for our sin. In the light of this supreme sacrifice, circumcision is irrelevant. What's important is faith.

Faith is about taking God at His Word. It's believing what He has to say about His Son. When we stand before the Lord, we don't think to ourselves, 'God will bless me because I'm "circumcised". I have a pious attitude to life and do many religious things. I go to church every Sunday, read my Bible, say my prayers and do good deeds for others. God is bound to honour me.'

No. We abandon our personal attempts at self-justification. We come to God and declare to Him, 'I have nothing to my credit. All my righteous acts are like filthy rags to you (see Isa. 64:6). But Jesus has died for me and has taken all my sins away. I stand here clothed in His righteousness. And because I'm trusting totally in Him, I can come to you with a clear conscience knowing that you will accept me.'

## ▓ To do

Put your love into practice today.

Do something special to bless someone you know.

## ▓ To meditate on

We must put faith to work.
'Let your light shine before men, that they may see your good deeds and praise your Father' (Matt. 5:16b).
'Let us consider how we may spur one another on towards love and good deeds' (Heb. 10:24).
'Live such good lives among the pagans that, though they accuse you of doing wrong, they may see your good deeds and glorify God on the day he visits us' (1 Pet. 2:12).

Faith alone saves you. But if you want your life to count for God, you will not be satisfied merely to have faith. You will begin to do things for God. The way to ensure that His blessing pursues you is to do what Paul says — put your faith to work through love.

Before someone believes in Jesus he is very self-centred and justifies all he does. He's convinced that he's right and will fight for his point of view. But when he's saved, he realises how dependent he is on Christ and instead of defending himself, he begins to reach out to others. Faith releases him to love.

His former antagonism is replaced by concern. He starts feeling sorry for people he once disliked. No longer is he consumed with bitterness towards those who've treated him unjustly. Instead, he's keen to bless his persecutors, to pray for his enemies and to serve those who hate him. He holds no grudges and gives all his unsolvable problems to God.

When people comment on the change in him, he says, 'I wasn't like this once. But I've put my faith in Jesus and He's made a difference to my life.' When people look at you, can they see your faith working through love?

## ▩ To reflect

Reflect on the changes there have been in your life since you became a Christian.

Would your colleagues/friends have noticed a difference?

Does love characterise your life?

What changes do you need to make to your lifestyle and/or attitudes to enable your faith to work through love?

**Devotion to God finds its outward expression in loving one another. Or, to state it another way, our devotion to God is validated by our love for other people.**
*Jerry Bridges*

# What race are you running?

You were running well; who hindered you from obeying the truth? This persuasion did not come from Him who calls you. A little leaven leavens the whole lump of dough. I have confidence in you in the Lord, that you will adopt no other view; but the one who is disturbing you shall bear his judgment, whoever he is (Gal. 5:7–10 NASB).

At one time the Galatians were running an excellent race. They were keen disciples of Jesus; they were enjoying His grace; they were happy. Then they succumbed to false teaching and veered off the track.

'What has happened to all your joy?' Paul asked them (Gal. 4:15a). Legalistic Christians always lose their joy. That's because they never think they've done enough to please God and consequently lack assurance of their salvation. You might think the more that legalistic Christians put themselves under law, the more they will obey God. The opposite is actually true. If you're trying to earn your salvation, you will become so tired of failing that you will end up more disobedient than ever.

Paul says that it takes only a little leaven to leaven the whole lump. A very small amount of yeast will have a profound effect on a large quantity of dough. Mix a tiny morsel of legalism into your Christian life and it will contaminate not just a part of your walk with God, but the whole of it.

It's interesting to note that Paul uses the illustration about leaven in two different ways. Here it refers to legalism, but in 1 Corinthians

## ▓ To ponder

What is the essential requirement if we are to please God? (See Heb. 11:6.)

_____

With this in mind can you say that your life is pleasing to God?

Yes/No

## ▓ To meditate on

Salvation brings joy.
'My lips will shout for joy when I sing praise to you — I, whom you have redeemed' (Ps. 71:23).
'He brought out his people with rejoicing, his chosen ones with shouts of joy' (Ps. 105:43).
'The LORD takes delights in his people; he crowns the humble with salvation. Let the saints rejoice in this honour and sing for joy on their beds' (Ps. 149:4,5).

5:6 it concerns careless living. The problems are total opposites. On the one hand you have Christians who are so eager to be godly that they impose rules on themselves to help them to please God more. On the other hand you have individuals who are so keen to avoid restrictions that they fall into sin. If you drift in either direction, you shipwreck your faith. The secret is to slip neither into legalism nor licence. And you do that by trusting solely in Christ and living to honour Him.

Paul knows that sincere Christians are always willing to hear the Word of God and obey it. That's why he has confidence that the Galatians will listen to him. He recognises that the false teachers have been convincing and understands the appeal of their message. The Galatians have become confused and have lost their way but Paul knows that they will change their minds when they hear the truth.

What will happen to the false teachers? Paul says that they will incur judgement. You may be theologically trained and in a position of prominence in the church, but if you're tampering with the gospel of Christ, you will never get away with it.

➤ Read Exodus 12:15,19; Matthew 13:33; 16:5–12.

➤ Write down in a notebook the different senses in which yeast is alluded to in each of these passages.

## ■ To assess

Describe in a notebook how you felt when you were first saved.

How do you feel now?

Has anything happened to change the way you feel?

The word *Christian* means different things to different people. To one person it means a stiff, uptight, inflexible way of life, colorless and unbending. To another it means a risky, surprise-filled venture, lived tiptoe at the edge of expectation.
*Eugene Peterson*

# The offence of the cross

But I, brethren, if I still preach circumcision, why am I still persecuted? Then the stumbling block of the cross has been abolished. Would that those who are troubling you would even mutilate themselves (Gal. 5:11,12 NASB).

It would seem that the false teachers in Galatia thought that Paul secretly agreed with their doctrine. 'He goes along with circumcision,' they were telling the believers. 'But he doesn't express his views publicly.'

Paul denied the rumour. 'If I'm preaching circumcision, why am I being persecuted?' he asked. You don't get opposed if you proclaim a moral gospel. People are happy if you say, 'Just do your best and you'll go to heaven.' But you're in real trouble if you declare, 'Your good works aren't good enough to please God. The only way of salvation is through the death and resurrection of Jesus.' That's a scandalous and deeply offensive message and you'll suffer for it.

Since Paul was still being persecuted, he could not have been telling people that they'd be saved through circumcision and lawkeeping. Had he proclaimed this kind of gospel, he would have removed the stumbling block of the cross. But he was preaching the true way of salvation and people didn't like it.

I can think of at least four reasons why the cross causes unbelievers to stumble. For a start, it's an ugly symbol. People don't like to think that their salvation rests on a man who

## ▓ To pray

Pray that the Lord will give you opportunities to witness for Him.

Aim to share the gospel with at least one person this week.

## ▓ To meditate on

Unbelievers stumble over the cross. 'The message of the cross is foolishness to those who are perishing, but to us who are being saved it is the power of God ... we preach Christ crucified: a stumbling-block to Jews and foolishness to Gentiles' (1 Cor. 1:18,23). 'But to those who do not believe, "The stone the builders rejected has become the capstone," and, "A stone that causes men to stumble and a rock that makes them fall"' (1 Pet. 2:7b,8a).

was crucified naked to a piece of wood. It's degrading to stoop to such a Saviour.

Secondly, people refuse to believe that Jesus was punished for them. Although Pilate and the centurion recognised that He was a righteous man, unbelievers generally don't want to acknowledge that He was innocent and that they are guilty. It's cuts across their pride to admit that His death was caused by their sins.

Thirdly, individuals dislike the idea that they can't contribute to their salvation. They want to trust in their own good works to gain favour with God. But the cross tells them that self-justification is useless, and that's offensive.

Then finally, people feel that they've got to add personal righteousness to Jesus' sacrifice in order to make themselves more acceptable to God. Like the Galatians they stumble on the cross because they can't believe that it releases them from all condemnation.

Paul's humour comes through when he suggests that the false teachers mutilate themselves. He's effectively saying, 'I wish that these people who want to circumcise others would use the knife on themselves.' It's Paul's way of utterly rejecting a legalistic gospel.

➤ Make sure that you know how to present the true gospel.

➤ Learn the following Scriptures or others you may choose.

- We are created in God's image, Genesis 1:27.
- Sin, Romans 3:23.
- God's love, John 3:16.
- Repent, Acts 2:38.
- Confess and believe, Romans 10:9.

➤ Explain the gospel to a Christian friend and ask them to comment on the clarity of your presentation.

## ▓ To answer

Look at the four reasons why the cross causes people to stumble.

In a notebook write down how you would deal with each of these in a discussion with a non-Christian.

The cross of Christ is the most revolutionary thing ever to appear among men ... We must do something about the cross, and one of two things only we can do— flee it or die upon it.
*A. W. Tozer*

## □ STUDY 8

# The law of love

For you were called to freedom, brethren; only do not turn your freedom into an opportunity for the flesh, but through love serve one another. For the whole Law is fulfilled in one word, in the statement, 'YOU SHALL LOVE YOUR NEIGHBOUR AS YOURSELF.' But if you bite and devour one another, take care lest you be consumed by one another (Gal. 5:13–15 NASB).

When Paul tells us that we've been called to freedom, he's summing up everything that he's said so far. 'You've finished with the law,' he effectively reminds us. 'When you died to the law your old self ceased to exist and a new person came into being. Now you must never let your sins accuse you. If you do wrong, you don't slip back into condemnation, you go to Jesus and He atones for you. You're free.'

At this point someone might ask, 'Isn't this a rather dangerous teaching? If I'm righteous for ever, I might as well sin as much as I like.' In response, Paul doesn't suddenly think, 'Wow! He's right. I'd better warn him that if he sins, God will pounce on him.' Why not? Because Paul doesn't want to point people back to the law and terrify them into obeying it.

Instead, he tells them, 'Don't misuse your freedom.' It isn't appropriate for Christians to sin as much as possible. If we're grateful to Jesus for what He's done for us, we won't take advantage of His grace. Rather, we'll voluntarily turn away from anything that displeases Him. Our motivation will be not law, but love.

Having pointed the Galatians away from the law, Paul shows them a way to fulfil it. He tells

## ▓ To question

How should we as Christians use our freedom?

_____

_____

_____

## ▓ To meditate on

Freedom promotes righteousness.
'What shall we say, then? Shall we go on sinning, so that grace may increase? By no means! We died to sin; how can we live in it any longer?' (Rom. 6:1,2)
'You have been set free from sin and have become slaves to righteousness' (Rom. 6:18).
'Live as free men, but do not use your freedom as a cover-up for evil; live as servants of God' (1 Pet. 2:16).

us that the law is fulfilled in the statement, 'You shall love your neighbour as yourself.' What he means is that if we live a life of love, we will automatically fulfil the law — even though we aren't under it.

When the Mosaic law declared, 'You shall not commit adultery, steal or give false testimony' it was taking a step towards the love that God really wants. The old Mosaic law is now too low a standard for us altogether. Its requirements are met but it altogether gets surpassed by Christian love.

Now that we're Christians, we don't obey the letter of the law on tablets of stone. We respond to the Spirit of love which is written in our hearts. There's something within us that tells us not to be impure, steal, lie or cheat. When we do any of these things, we feel bad about it. Instinctively we know that we have been called to love one another. And when we do this, we fulfil the law of Moses almost without trying.

In fact, love takes us beyond the law. It prompts us to pray for our enemies and relate kindly to those who misuse us. It draws us away from petty church squabbles and promotes harmony and joy.

## ▓ To list

What does it mean to love yourself?

List practical ways in which we can love our neighbour as ourself.

_____

_____

_____

_____

## ▓ Food for thought

➤ Read Jeremiah 31:31–34 (Hebrews 8:8–13); Ezekiel 11:18–20.

➤ Write down the common theme which runs through these passages.

_____

_____

➤ How is the New Covenant different from the Old Covenant?

_____

There are but two loves, love of ourselves and love of God and of others. To live is to choose between these two loves.
_Michel Quoist_

# The flesh and the Spirit

But I say, walk by the Spirit, and you will not carry out the desire of the flesh. For the flesh sets its desire against the Spirit, and the Spirit against the flesh; for these are in opposition to one another, so that you may not do the things that you please. But if you are led by the Spirit, you are not under the Law (Gal. 5:16–18 NASB).

The Holy Spirit lives in every Christian, so Paul can exhort us, 'Walk by the Spirit.' The Spirit will prompt us to live in a godly way and we must respond to Him on a daily basis.

Paul not only takes for granted the presence of the Spirit in our lives, he also refers to the flesh. Now sometimes 'flesh' means 'human nature' — Jesus became flesh (John 1:14). Sometimes it means 'unregenerate nature' — as in the case of an unconverted person. And sometimes it means a 'desire to sin' — which is what Christians experience.

When we believe in Jesus, He makes us a new person who wants to live righteously. The Spirit says, 'Live for the glory of God' and our hearts reply, 'Yes, I want to do that.' But the fact that we're Christians doesn't make us incapable of sin. So while the Spirit encourages us to behave in a godly way, the flesh tugs us in the opposite direction and tempts us to give in to all sorts of ungodliness. If we walk by the Spirit, the natural consequence is that we will not fulfil the desires of the flesh.

Now we might say to ourselves, 'I feel condemned by certain evil desires and wish I could deal with sin once and for all.' Paul

## ▓ To outline

'What does it mean to walk after the Spirit? ... Firstly, it is not a work; it is a walk.' *Watchman Nee.*

In your notebook outline the differences between a work and a walk.

## ▓ To meditate on

Consistency must be on a daily basis.
'The days of the blameless are known to the LORD' (Ps. 37:18a).
'(I will) fulfil my vows day after day' (Ps. 61:8b).
'Teach us to number our days aright, that we may gain a heart of wisdom' (Ps. 90:12).
'Whoever would love life and see good days must keep his tongue from evil and his lips from deceitful speech' (1 Pet. 3:10).

addresses this problem by saying, 'If you are led by the Spirit, you are not under the Law.' In other words, 'If you are experiencing a battle with sin, it means that you're conscious of the Spirit's desires and this confirms that you're saved. This, in turn, implies that you're not under law and must therefore refuse to succumb to feelings of condemnation.'

Some Christians wonder which is going to win — Spirit or flesh. Paul puts the onus on us. 'Walk by the Spirit,' he declares. The Spirit isn't going to force us to act appropriately. 'I (not the Spirit) can do everything through him who gives me strength' (Phil. 4:13) says Paul. The Spirit gives us the power to resist all temptation, but we've got to do the resisting.

It isn't sufficient to shrug off responsibility and say, 'I'm praying about it, asking God to deal with my fleshly desires.' God won't just remove sin. We must 'put to death the misdeeds of the body' (Rom. 8:13b). The side that wins is the one we follow. If we go for the flesh, it will have an increasing grip on our lives. If we yield to the Spirit, we will overcome the enemy, grow in our knowledge of God and experience His blessing on everything we do.

➤ Write in a notebook a modern-day parable (word-picture) to illustrate the difference between the flesh and the Spirit.

## ▓ To pray

'Be filled with the Spirit' (Eph. 5:18b).

We should be constantly drawing on the Spirit's resources.

Make it your aim to pray every day for the filling of the Holy Spirit.

The Christian is one who is even dead to his old self, to his old nature, to that condition which he inherited from Adam ... We have been given a new nature. We have finished with the old self once and for all. We are now in Christ.
*D. Martyn Lloyd-Jones*

# Lead us not into temptation

Now the deeds of the flesh are evident (Gal. 5:19a NASB).

It's significant that Paul lists the deeds of the flesh before he mentions the fruit of the Spirit. This is because we must deal with our fleshly desires before we can grow in godliness. If we're full of strife, jealousy or anger, we will never be able to cultivate love, kindness or self-control. We must conquer the one before we can engage in the other.

Unbelievers can't handle sin because they're slaves to it. But when they're converted, they become slaves to righteousness (Rom. 6:17,18) and have the power of the Spirit to overcome temptation. Now we may think it surprising that Paul feels it necessary to warn Christians not to indulge in certain sinful practices. 'Can a believer really fall into immorality, idolatry, drunkenness, carousing and sins like that?' we may ask. Well, Paul obviously thought so — otherwise he wouldn't have mentioned them.

Some believers overestimate their strength and confidently assert, 'I could never fall into that kind of sin.' Then they become careless and start fooling around with temptation. One day they find themselves doing the very thing they thought that they would always be able to resist. Paul says, 'If you think you are standing

## ▓ To research

Name, in a notebook, three Bible characters who yielded to temptation.

What was their sin?

What happened to them?

## ▓ To meditate on

We need not fall into temptation. 'Watch and pray so that you will not fall into temptation. The spirit is willing, but the body is weak' (Matt. 26:41). 'Because he himself suffered when he was tempted, he is able to help those who are being tempted' (Heb. 2:18). 'For we do not have a high priest who is unable to sympathise with our weaknesses, but we have one who has been tempted in every way, just as we are — yet was without sin' (Heb. 4:15).

firm, be careful that you don't fall' (1 Cor. 10:12b). Let's consistently recognise how subtle sin can be and steer clear of it.

'But,' say a number of Christians, 'no one has ever faced this temptation before. I can't possibly conquer it because it's far too strong for me.' Well, the Bible confidently declares that the temptations you face are not unique — they're 'common to man' (1 Cor. 10:13b). So you can't say, 'It's impossible for me to resist this temptation' — because others have resisted it before you.

When a temptation is particularly severe, it's easy to think, 'This temptation is more than I can bear. I can't handle it.' That's not true. God won't let you be tempted beyond your strength and promises to provide you with a way of escape (1 Cor. 10:13). The devil may whisper, 'You can't possibly turn away from this sin,' but God declares that you can.

The Bible says, 'Do not let sin reign in your mortal body' (Rom. 6:12a). It tells you that you have mastery over temptation. The Spirit wants to help you in this. Identify your areas of greatest weakness, submit to God, resist the devil and he will flee from you (James 4:7).

➢ Read and memorise James 1:13–15.

➢ How do these verses contradict such phrases as 'the Devil made me do it,' and 'I couldn't help myself'?

➢ Who *is* responsible for sin in our lives?

## ▓ To identify

Identify three areas of weakness in your life.

_____

_____

What practical steps can you take to keep yourself from temptation in these areas?

_____

_____

To experience practical, everyday holiness, we must accept the fact that God in His infinite wisdom has seen fit to allow this daily battle with indwelling sin. But God does not leave us to do battle alone. Just as He delivered us from the overall reign of sin, so He has made ample provision for us to win the daily skirmishes against sin.
*Jerry Bridges*

# Sexual sin

Now the deeds of the flesh are evident, which are: immorality, impurity, sensuality (Gal. 5:19 NASB).

The first three 'deeds of the flesh' that Paul mentions are all connected with sexual sin. The Bible speaks very positively about a sexual relationship within marriage, but outside that context it is totally inappropriate. Here Paul is referring to sins like adultery, fornication and homosexuality. Our flesh may want to engage in such practices but they are out of bounds where God is concerned.

Maybe you have an ongoing problem with sexual temptation. You may be so embarrassed that you haven't dared talk to anyone about it, but you really wish that you could break free. It's possible that you haven't actually done anything wrong with your body, but you know that you commit sins in your imagination. I'd like to share three principles to help you.

Firstly, if you are a Christian you can handle sexual temptation — even if you don't feel that you can. Jesus was tempted in every way — which implies that He encountered sexual temptation. He sympathises with you because He knows from personal experience exactly how you feel. But He also shows from personal experience that you can resist sinful desires if you draw on His strength.

## ▓ To memorise

Memorise 1 Corinthians 6:19, 20.

'Do you not know that your body is a temple of the Holy Spirit, who is in you, whom you have received from God? You are not your own; you were bought at a price. Therefore honour God with your body.'

## ▓ To meditate on

God's power is there to help.
'My grace is sufficient for you, for my power is made perfect in weakness" (2 Cor. 12:9b).
'(He is) able to do immeasurably more than all we ask or imagine, according to his power that is at work within us' (Eph. 3:20).
'Live a life worthy of the Lord ... being strengthened with all power according to his glorious might so that you may have great endurance' (Col. 1:10b,11a).

Secondly, resisting sin is always painful. If you have become trapped in a habit, getting out of it is going to be hard. If you've done something a thousand times and you say to yourself, 'Next time I'm going to resist this,' you'll be in for a battle. Your flesh will scream out for satisfaction and you'll be tempted to give in almost before you've started. But let me tell you something encouraging: the first time you resist will be very painful, but the next time it will be easier and the next, easier still. Once you get used to resisting, you will have broken the habit. That's how it works.

Thirdly, learn to deal with sin before it takes hold of you. Cut it dead at its source. Refuse to go to places where you might succumb to sexual sin. Don't read anything that might stimulate your imagination. Don't have friends who might lead you into immorality. Don't be alone late at night with a girlfriend or boyfriend.

If you play with fire, you will get burnt and if you fool around with temptation, it will bring about your downfall. If you want to overcome sin you can. Jesus is your great high priest and His Spirit has the power to see you through the pain and into freedom and victory.

➤ The church has sometimes alienated people with its preaching against fornication and immorality.

➤ Write down in a notebook how you would explain this message to a non-Christian friend.

## ▓ To pray

Spend some time before the Lord; confess any involvement in sexual sin; ask the Lord to give you a healthy attitude towards sex and to keep you from temptation.

Jesus gives us moral laws not to undercut our enjoyment of life and frustrate us ... but ... because *He loves us and desires to discipline us in a way that will best bring us into the fullness of all life has to offer.*
Larry Tomczak

# Idolatry and sorcery

Now the deeds of the flesh are evident, which are: ... idolatry, sorcery (Gal. 5:19a,20a NASB).

I n the Scriptures, idolatry is often mentioned in the same context as sexual sin. Paul warns the Corinthians, 'Do not be idolaters' and immediately adds, 'We should not commit sexual immorality' (1 Cor. 10:7a,8a).

God forbids idolatry — the setting up of something which we think will help us to worship Him. In its crudest sense, this involves the manufacture of a metal, wooden or stone image which is specifically designed to be revered (e.g. Exod. 32:2–4; Acts 19:27,35).

But there are more subtle forms of idolatry. In order to help us worship God we can start using things like pictures, statues, beads or candles. The problem here is that the object which is meant to enhance our worship of God soon becomes the focus of our adulation. We start by praising Jesus through a picture and end up praying to the picture itself.

Then of course we are guilty of idolatry when we give God second place in our affections. We may idolise a person — be that a pop star, a relation, or a friend. Or we may worship a possession — our home, our car, or our money. We may not be conscious of what we're doing until God challenges us about it.

## ▓ To answer

What does it mean to worship in Spirit and in truth?

_____

_____

_____

## ▓ To meditate on

Jesus must take first place.
'Seek first his kingdom and his righteousness' (Matt. 6:33b).
'I hold this against you: You have forsaken your first love' (Rev. 2:4).
'He is the beginning and the firstborn from among the dead, so that in everything he might have the supremacy' (Col. 1:18b).
'God exalted him to the highest place and gave him the name that is above every name' (Phil 2:9b).

The flesh is weak. It tries to draw us away from God and into a preoccupation with things. We prefer to worship what we can see when God wants us to worship without visual aids. The only two visible signs that He gives us to stimulate our worship are baptism and the Lord's Supper. But apart from these, we must learn how to worship Him not in sight and touch but in Spirit and truth (John 4:23).

After idolatry comes sorcery — seeking contact with the supernatural through other means than the gospel of Christ. Many people want to experience the paranormal. They may wish to contact the dead or find supernatural guidance or answers to prayer. So they go to a medium, a clairvoyant, a spiritualist, a faith healer, a fortune teller, or some such person. They may be convinced that these people are genuine but are, in fact, deceived.

Jesus wants to bless us in supernatural ways. But so often our flesh prompts us to seek the supernatural without submitting our lives to His Word. Christians who are lax about their relationship with Jesus and who crave spiritual experiences are teetering on the edge of sorcery.

## ▓ To consider

Are there any idols in your life?

Ask the Lord to show you if any of your possessions or relationships are coming between you and Him.

## ▓ Food for thought

➤ Read Leviticus 19:31; 20:6,27; Deuteronomy 18:9–13; 2 Kings 21; 1 Chronicles 10:13.

➤ Notice the severity of God's wrath.

➤ What implications does this have for our *New Age* generation?

The Lord, who has betrothed us to Himself in truth, declares that He burns with the hottest jealousy whenever, neglecting the purity of His holy marriage, we defile ourselves with abominable lusts, and especially when the worship of His deity, which ought to have been most carefully kept unimpaired, is transferred to another, or adulterated with some superstition.
*John Calvin*

# Enmity, strife and jealousy

Now the deeds of the flesh are evident, which are: ... enmities, strife, jealousy
(Gal. 5:19a,20b NASB).

The next eight 'deeds of the flesh' that Paul mentions are sins of attitude. They concern the way in which we relate to people.

**Enmities** is the first of these. Sometimes we're tempted to become argumentative and irritable. We look at others and start resenting their success. Then we become hostile towards them and begin to hold grudges. In addition, we justify ourselves and refuse to admit our guilt. 'Everyone else is wrong and I'm right,' we declare. 'They've got to change, not me.' Needless to say, such an attitude as this will destroy a marriage.

Paul mentions **strife** next because it relates to enmity. If you have a hostile spirit, you will become quarrelsome — which is exactly what characterises strife. So when people speak to you, your immediate reaction will be to argue with them. It doesn't matter what they say, you will find some objection to it. You will gain a reputation as someone who constantly protests and focuses on the worst things that people do.

Your never-ending criticisms may have their roots in a sense of personal worthlessness. In other words, you have to drag others down in order to pull yourself up. For this reason, it's

## ▓ To repent

Repent of any bad attitudes you have towards anyone.

Find some way of blessing them this week.

## ▓ To meditate on

We mustn't be jealous or quarrelsome. 'Since there is jealousy and quarrelling among you, are you not worldly? Are you not acting like mere men?'
(1 Cor. 3:3b)
'What causes fights and quarrels among you? Don't they come from your desires that battle within you? You want something but don't get it. You kill and covet, but you cannot have what you want. You quarrel and fight'
(James 4:1,2a).

no wonder that Paul mentions **jealousy** after strife since a competitive spirit will inevitably lead to rivalry.

Although people tend to be willing to admit hostility towards someone, few are prepared to say, 'I'm jealous of him/her.' But the root of hostility may in fact be jealousy. There's that colleague at work. His output is far greater than yours and everyone appreciates him more than you — and he's not even a Christian! So you begin to resent him and look for faults in everything he does.

A characteristic of jealousy is that it often affects people who are close — work colleagues, family members or best friends. You may be jealous of someone's success, his wealth, his possessions, his influence, his popularity, his appearance, his charisma or even his devotion to God. If you were honest, what you really want is to be like him.

We mustn't justify these attitudes saying, 'I can't help it. That's the way I was made.' As far as God is concerned, enmities, strife and jealousy are 'deeds of the flesh' which we must confront, identify as wrong and overcome in the strength that He will supply.

> ➤ Read 1 Samuel 18.
>
> ➤ Identify any enmity, strife or jealousy in David and Saul's relationship.

### ▓ To challenge

Read Philippians 2:14.

Is this your testimony?

Write down in a notebook three practical steps you can take towards achieving this command and put them into practice.

> When you look at someone with eyes of love, you see a reality different from that of someone who looks at the same person without love, with hatred or even just with indifference.
> *Desmond Tutu*

# Anger, disputes, etc.

Now the deeds of the
flesh are evident, which
are: ... outbursts of
anger, disputes,
dissensions, factions,
envying, drunkenness,
carousing and things
like these
(Gal. 5:19a,20b,21a
NASB).

**P**aul adds **outbursts of anger** to his list of 'deeds of the flesh'. Some people have a real problem controlling their tempers. Something happens and they flare up in a moment, then later they try to convince themselves that their outburst was justified.

One Scriptural example of this kind of anger occurred in the synagogue in Nazareth. Jesus was preaching to the people who became so furious at what He said that they drove Him out of town (Luke 4:28–30). Paul experienced similar animosity in Ephesus when he challenged the existence of man-made gods. So enraged were the Ephesians that they started a riot in the city (Acts 19:27,28).

The word **disputes** can be translated 'selfish ambition' (NIV) and it refers to a desire to manipulate. Many of us want to get our own way. So we push ourselves forward and force others to hear our opinions. But this isn't the biblical route to exaltation. If you want God to use you powerfully, you must be humble — just as Jesus was.

**Dissensions** occur when people take their eyes off Jesus and forget that they're living for Him. They get sidetracked by a particular

## ▓ To question

What are the characteristics of a humble person?

_____

_____

How can you humble yourself?

_____

_____

## ▓ To meditate on

Exaltation comes through humility.
'The Lord ... humbles and he exalts'
(1 Sam. 2:7).
'No-one ... can exalt a man. But it is
God who judges: He brings one down,
he exalts another' (Ps. 75:6,7).
'Whoever exalts himself will be
humbled, and whoever humbles
himself will be exalted' (Matt. 23:12b).
'Humble yourselves, therefore, under
God's mighty hand, that he may lift
you up in due time' (1 Pet. 5:6).

quarrel or conviction and form a distinct group around it. They usually have a leader and separate themselves from other Christians.

The result of dissensions are 'factions'. The group members begin to judge another person in terms of whether or not he belongs to the group. 'Is he in our denomination?' they say. 'Does he follow our theology? What evangelistic techniques does he use? How does he view baptism or the Holy Spirit?'

The main problem with these people is a selfish preoccupation with their own viewpoint. They become so concerned about preserving the cause of their little group that they become argumentative and elitist. Then they lose sight of the Cross, fail to reach out with the love of God and forget that they're meant to be engaged in establishing the Kingdom.

Next Paul mentions **envying** which creeps over you when others are blessed and you aren't. **Drunkenness** is the misuse of alcohol and it results in 'carousing' — involvement in noisy or lively drinking parties.

'Don't gratify these desires,' Paul pleads with us. They will seek to have mastery over us; we mustn't give in to them.

➤ Read 1 Corinthians 3:1–9. What was happening in Corinth?

➤ Do you see any evidence of this kind of behaviour in your church?

➤ Read John 17:20,21.

➤ Spend time praying for Christian unity as described in these verses.

## ▨ To consider

What is your attitude towards alcohol?

On what Scriptures do you base your standpoint?

_____

_____

_____

To become effective in our interactions with people, we must change in our approach to relationships. We must turn from self-protective maneuvering to a rich involvement that deeply touches people. And that turn occurs only through repentance.
*Dr Larry Crabb*

# Inheriting the Kingdom

... of which I forewarn you just as I have forewarned you that those who practice such things shall not inherit the kingdom of God
(Gal. 5:21b NASB).

H aving listed the 'deeds of the flesh' Paul goes on to warn us that those who practise them will not inherit the Kingdom of God. What does he mean by that?

Is he saying, 'People who've been guilty of things like impurity, idolatry, strife and anger can't become Christians'? No, because Jesus Himself declares, 'all the sins and blasphemies of men will be forgiven them' (Mark 3:28b).

Is he saying, 'People who fall into these sins were never Christians in the first place'? No, he can't mean that either. He wouldn't be telling believers, 'Don't do that' if they were incapable of doing it. Indeed, we know from experience that believers are sometimes guilty of sin. They become careless and slip into things like selfishness, bitterness or jealousy.

Is he saying, 'People who commit these sins lose their salvation'? No, because John tells us that if we confess our sins, God will forgive us and purify us (1 John 1:9). So what does Paul mean when he speaks about our failing to inherit the Kingdom?

To explain what he's getting at, let's look at an Old Testament illustration. The Israelites were redeemed by the blood of the Passover

## ▓ To define

Define what it means to have a damaged inheritance.

Write down three examples.

_____

_____

_____

## ▓ To meditate on

We inherit the Kingdom progressively. 'We must go through many hardships to enter the kingdom of God' (Acts 14:22b).
'The wicked will not inherit the kingdom of God' (1 Cor. 6:9b).
'We do not want you to become lazy, but to imitate those who through faith and patience inherit what has been promised' (Heb. 6:12).
'We are receiving a kingdom that cannot be shaken' (Heb. 12:28b).

Lamb and their salvation was marked by their exodus from Egypt. But that wasn't the end of the story. God had saved them not so that they could wander around in the desert, but so that they could conquer their enemies and inherit all the territory of Canaan.

Similarly, when we become Christians, we effectively step through the front door of the Kingdom. But that's only the beginning of the journey. God doesn't want us to amble round aimlessly, but to enter into all the blessings that He has for us. The expression, 'inherit the Kingdom' sometimes refers to salvation, but not always. Here it means that if we're complacent about our Christianity and indulge in various sins we will damage our inheritance.

Maybe you've become casual about your walk with God. You tolerate sin and think that it isn't doing you any harm. Well, you're robbing yourself of your inheritance. If you're brutally honest, you will have to admit that you aren't experiencing the joy of your salvation or a deep intimacy with the Lord. If you continue to resist God, you will never inherit the Kingdom, but if you deal with your sin — whatever that costs — God will pour His blessings on your life.

➢ Read Deuteronomy 28:1–14.

➢ Write out in a notebook each of the blessings God promises to His people and set them in a modern context.

➢ Are you experiencing these blessings?

➢ What is the condition attached to receiving the blessings?

■ **To memorise**

Memorise Psalm 66:18.

'If I had cherished sin in my heart, the Lord would not have listened.'

It is therefore the church's duty to display in an evil age of self-seeking, pride, and animosity the life and fellowship of the Kingdom of God and of the age to come. This display of Kingdom life is an essential element in the witness of the church to the Kingdom of God.
*George Eldon Ladd*

# The fruit of the Spirit

But the fruit of the Spirit
is ... (Gal. 5:22a NASB).

When Paul has finished talking about the 'deeds of the flesh' he turns to the 'fruit of the Spirit'. But why does he change the word 'deeds' to 'fruit'?

Well, the deeds of the flesh come easily to us. We don't have to be taught how to entertain impure thoughts, or hold resentment, or get angry. If we give these things room, they will come quite naturally to us. There's a directness about them.

The thing about the fruit of the Spirit is that it's produced indirectly. We cannot create love, joy and peace any more than we can manufacture an apple, a pear or a banana. These attributes come not from us but from the Spirit. We sow a seed which grows into a tree and then that tree eventually produces the fruit. So a deed is something that has an immediate effect while a fruit develops over a period of time (2 Cor 3:18).

We become fruitful not as we strive to be good, but as we submit to the Holy Spirit. We obey Him, He produces the fruit within us and we grow in godliness. Although righteousness and justification come immediately at conversion, Christlikeness is a lifelong process.

## ▒ To ponder

What has the Holy Spirit been saying to you recently?

_____

How have you responded to this?

_____

## ▒ To meditate on

God wants to make us fruitful.
'Produce fruit in keeping with repentance' (Matt. 3:8).
'He cuts off every branch in me that bears no fruit, while every branch that does bear fruit he prunes so that it will be even more fruitful' (John 15:2).
'The fruit of the light consists in all goodness, righteousness and truth' (Eph. 5:9).
'Be ... filled with the fruit of righteousness' (Phil. 1:11a).

If we want to be like Jesus, we must stop listening to our fleshly desires which promise us immediate satisfaction. And we must learn to be sensitive to the Holy Spirit who will give us far deeper fulfilment. He will speak to us through the Word, through people, through circumstances or through an inner witness.

The Bible warns us, 'Today, if you hear his voice, do not harden your hearts' (Heb. 4:7b) — which means that it's possible to resist the voice of the Spirit and to hinder the growth of the fruit in our lives. It's up to every individual believer to determine, 'I will respond to Him whatever He says to me.'

Let's also notice that the Greek word that Paul uses for 'fruit' is singular. The things that we must cultivate in our lives are not separate, they belong together as a group.

Now 'love' comes first because it's the key to everything else that he mentions. If you don't demonstrate love, you will never be joyful, peaceful, patient and so on. It's useless saying, 'Lord, make me a kinder person' if you're unloving. A love for others will naturally make you kind to them, so you must pursue love first and everything else will follow.

➤ Using a whole page of your notebook draw a diagram of a tree showing its roots below the ground.

➤ Look up the following verses and write them in at the relevant places on your diagram:

Isaiah 61:3b; Psalm 1:3; 104:16a; Galatians 5:22,23; Ephesians 3:17.

➤ Use this diagram as an aide-memoire when you pray about your own spiritual growth.

## ▩ To assess

'But grow in the grace and knowledge of our Lord and Saviour Jesus Christ' (2 Pet. 3:18).

How do we grow as Christians?

Assess what growth there has been in your life since you became a Christian and thank God for it.

**God grant that within us there might be generated an enormous, overwhelming, irresistible desire to become like Him who is *love*... to have reproduced in us the fruit of His life.**
*W. Phillip Keller*

# Love

> But the fruit of the Spirit is love
> (Gal. 5:22a NASB).

> Love is patient, love is kind, and is not jealous; love does not brag and is not arrogant, does not act unbecomingly; it does not seek its own, is not provoked, does not take into account a wrong suffered, does not rejoice in unrighteousness, but rejoices with the truth; bears all things, believes all things, hopes all things, endures all things. Love never fails
> (1 Cor. 13:4–8a NASB).

God wants us to love one another. We've already touched on this subject, but to do it justice we must go to the supreme passage on love — 1 Corinthians 13. Here Paul explains love in four different contexts.

Firstly he imagines a situation in which we've been ill treated and want to lash out at the person who's responsible. But love doesn't seek revenge and gnash its teeth enviously at the happy state of the wicked. It's patient and kind and refuses to be drawn into jealousy.

Secondly, Paul refers to an occasion when we are in a position of superiority and are tempted to look down on those who are under us and order them around. But love doesn't brag and it isn't arrogant, it doesn't act unbecomingly and it doesn't seek its own way.

Thirdly, Paul speaks about a context in which we are in an inferior position. Maybe someone in a more senior role is getting the credit for what we're doing. We look at this injustice and feel deeply angry about it. But love isn't provoked and it overlooks wrongs. It may recognise unrighteousness, but it doesn't slip down unrighteous paths. Instead, it rejoices with the truth.

## ▓ To ascertain

Read 1 Peter 4:8.

Ascertain what this verse really means.

(Is sin to be overlooked?)

## ▓ To meditate on

God has called us to love each other. 'Love each other as I have loved you. Greater love has no-one than this, that he lay down his life for his friends' (John 15:12b,13).
'Do everything in love' (1 Cor. 16:14).
'May the Lord make your love increase and overflow for each other and for everyone else' (1 Thess. 3:12a).

Finally, Paul focuses on a situation when we might be drawn into opposing others. We see someone doing something that we think is wrong and we're quick to judge him, 'How terrible!' we say. But it may be possible to interpret the person's action in more than one way. The trouble is that we have a natural bias towards attributing the worst possible motives.

Love bears all things. It doesn't get hostile but accepts that people aren't perfect. Love believes all things. It thinks the very best of everyone and readily excuses their faults. Love hopes all things. When it sees someone doing something 'wrong' it doesn't abandon him as a hopeless case. Rather, it looks forward to his improving and prays God's greatest blessing on his life. It treats its worst enemies as though they were its best friends.

Love endures all things. When you can't do anything about your situation, you don't try to take revenge, you endure hardship and leave the situation in the hands of God. He may vindicate you now or on the day of judgement. That's not your concern. You just show love — the quality of love that only the Holy Spirit can produce in you, the love that never fails.

➤ Imagine that you are discipling a new Christian.

➤ How would you teach them to reach out in a loving way towards those around them?

➤ What practical assignments could you give them?

## ▨ To do

Write down in a notebook four examples of how we can lay down our life for our friends.

Choose one of these and seek to put it into practice as soon as you can.

It must be emphasized ... that I have the love of God only to the extent that I have God Himself. God does not dispense the fruits of His Spirit apart from Himself!
*W. Phillip Keller*

# Joy, peace, patience ...

But the fruit of the Spirit is ... joy, peace, patience, kindness, goodness (Gal. 5:22 NASB).

As we practise love we will experience the other aspects of the fruit of the Spirit. The first of these is joy.

After the Ethiopian eunuch had become a Christian he 'went on his way rejoicing' (Acts 8:39b). That's a characteristic of anyone who trusts in Jesus. The wonder of having your sins forgiven wells up and bubbles over in joy.

But here Paul isn't only talking about the joy that accompanies salvation, he's referring to the joy that follows love. When we're vindictive and quarrelsome, we feel uneasy inside and out of sorts with God. But if we reach out in loving ways towards others, we know that God is pleased which, in turn, makes us feel happy.

Salvation brings peace. We read, 'Since we have been justified through faith, we have peace with God' (Rom. 5:1b). If we sin against God or against others, we will lose our peace and experience strife instead. The Bible warns us, 'There is no peace ... for the wicked' (Isa. 48:22). But if we keep ourselves from sin and love others in practical ways, we will continue to know an inner sense of peace.

Patience comes next in Paul's list. It refers to our being slow to get angry. If we are keen to

## ▩ To pray

Submit yourself to God and ask Him to produce the character of Jesus in you.

Write down in a notebook anything the Lord tells you to do and make sure you obey Him.

## ▩ To meditate on

God has the power to renew us.
'Do not conform any longer to the pattern of this world, but be transformed by the renewing of your mind' (Rom. 12.2a).
'Though outwardly we are wasting away, yet inwardly we are being renewed day by day' (2 Cor. 4:16).
'You have ... put on the new self, which is being renewed in knowledge in the image of its Creator' (Col. 3:9b,10a).

express love, we won't lose our temper when things go against us or become impatient with people who annoy us. Rather, we will overcome our feelings of frustration and be considerate towards others.

Kindness is the opposite of things like roughness, harshness and aggressiveness. It's so easy to treat people more severely than they deserve. 'Look what you've done now!' we say. Then we impose the maximum penalty for this crime and all others that the individual ever commits. But if we're kind, we'll do whatever we can to make someone feel accepted rather than pounce on his sin.

Goodness is about being upright and godly. Many Christians live in compromise. They measure their progress by worldly standards of goodness and forgive themselves for things that God would call sin. He's looking for believers who reject any hint of unrighteousness and who live according to His Word.

We may consider the weak areas in our lives and think, 'I can't possibly change that'. But the fruit is not 'of us' but 'of the Spirit'. As we submit to Him, He will produce the character of Jesus that God so longs to see in each of us.

> ➤ Aim to read a Christian biography over the next week or two.
>
> ➤ As you do so make a note of every evidence of the fruit of the Spirit in the life of the subject.

## ▨ To study

Write down examples from Scripture which illustrate God's love, joy, peace, patience, kindness and goodness.

_____

_____

_____

_____

The secret is not 'imitation' (Christians imitating Christ's life) so much as 'reproduction' (Christ reproducing his life through us). It is not just that we see the glory of Jesus by the illumination of the Holy Spirit, but that we are being changed into the image of Jesus by the indwelling power of the Holy Spirit.
_John Stott_

# Faithfulness, gentleness ...

But the fruit of the Spirit is ... faithfulness, gentleness, self-control; against such things there is no law (Gal. 5:22,23 NASB).

The next fruit that Paul mentions is faithfulness. Can God trust us to do what He asks of us? Do people see us as thoroughly reliable or hopelessly untrustworthy? Do we readily deceive others and resort to lying? Do we keep our promises? If we say we'll do something, can people rely on us? Are we trustworthy at work, in our friendships, in our marriage and in our service for the church?

Gentleness can be translated 'meekness' and it has to do with our not rushing to defend ourselves. Moses was described as the meekest man on earth (Num. 12:3). When people rose up against him, he didn't retaliate in anger. He left his vindication to God. We must come to the point where we don't feel that we have to protect our reputation all the time. When others criticise us, we refuse to expend untold energy trying to prove our innocence. Rather we respond with gentle humility and allow God to work out His plans for our lives.

The final fruit is self-control — which means that we have ourselves in check. When someone annoys us we don't lose our temper. We refuse to over-indulge in food or drink. We restrict our spending to match our income. And

## ▓ To demonstrate

Meekness is often equated with weakness.

Demonstrate that the opposite is true using examples from the life of Jesus.

## ▓ To meditate on

We have a better covenant.
'Jesus has become the guarantee of a better covenant' (Heb. 7:22b).
'The ministry Jesus has received is as superior to theirs as the covenant of which he is mediator is superior to the old one, and it is founded on better promises' (Heb. 8:6b).
'He has made us competent as ministers of a new covenant — not of the letter but of the Spirit; for the letter kills, but the Spirit gives life' (2 Cor. 3:6).

we maintain a tight reign on our tongue when we could say unkind things to or about others.

We need to control our minds too. The Holy Spirit doesn't want us to consider unholy things. Do you ever fantasise about committing sexual sin? You don't actually do anything, but you entertain the thoughts. Or maybe you hold a mental argument with someone you don't like. Or perhaps you think about being wealthy or famous. Secretly you want public acclaim and you hold imaginary conversations with famous people who tell you how great you are.

Right at the end of the list, Paul tells us that there is no law against the fruit of the Spirit. Sometimes he emphasises a point by putting it negatively. 'I am ... a citizen of no ordinary city' he said (Acts 21:39b). And 'I am not ashamed of the gospel' (Rom. 1:16a). What he meant was, 'It's a great city' and 'I'm proud of the gospel.'

So when he declares, 'Against such things there is no law' he's really saying, 'These things are better than anything that the law could do.' The law of Moses could never produce love, joy, peace and so on — so it's pointless putting yourself under it. The way of the Spirit is better by far.

> ➤ Write a Psalm describing God's faithfulness and thanking Him for it.

## ▓ To analyse

Do you have yourself in check?

In which area is your self-control weakest?

_____

_____

Plan a strategy for working on this and review your progress in a fortnight's time.

The *incentive* to exhibit these fine traits of character (the fruit of the Spirit) was furnished by Christ, for it is out of gratitude to him that believers adorn their conduct with them.
*William Hendriksen*

# Draw near to God

Now those who belong to Christ Jesus have crucified the flesh with its passions and desires. If we live by the Spirit, let us also walk by the Spirit
(Gal. 5:24,25 NASB).

When Paul tells us that 'Those who belong to Christ Jesus have crucified the flesh,' what does he mean? He could be referring to conversion when we begin the process of resisting sin. But I tend to prefer an alternative view.

The emphasis may be on the people who 'belong'. In other words, those who are close to Jesus are the ones who have crucified the flesh. They've resisted unholy passions and desires and are living blamelessly before God. As a direct result of this, He draws very near to them and blesses them in a special way.

Holiness reaps a reward. If you consistently refuse to allow the deeds of the flesh to get a grip on your life, you will increasingly 'belong' to Christ. He will effectively look at you and say, 'There's someone who can be trusted to follow me on a day-to-day basis, so I'm going to pour out my blessing on him and use him more and more.' Even in this life He whispers into your heart, 'Well done, good and faithful servant.'

Paul continues, 'If we live by the Spirit, let us also walk by the Spirit.' The first of these two phrases is an assumption. Paul is assuming that he's talking to believers who, because of

## ▓ To consider

Drawing near to God will inevitably involve time — time to pray, time to study, time to meditate, time in His presence.

Consider how much time you are devoting to drawing near to God.

What adjustments could you make to enable you to spend more time with the Lord?

## ▓ To meditate on

We are alive to God by faith in Christ. 'I have been crucified with Christ and I no longer live, but Christ lives in me. The life I live in the body, I live by faith in the Son of God' (Gal. 2:20).
'He redeemed us ... so that by faith we might receive the promise of the Spirit' (Gal. 3:14b).
'God, who is rich in mercy, made us alive with Christ even when we were dead in transgrassions — it is by grace you have been saved' (Eph. 2:4b,5).

the new birth, are alive through the Holy Spirit. The word 'if' could be translated 'since'. It expresses not doubt but confidence.

The second phrase is an appeal. Paul is saying, 'Since we really are alive to the Spirit, let's walk by the Spirit.' The word 'walk' in verse 25 is different from the word translated 'walk' in verse 16. Here the Greek has a more exact meaning, namely 'to keep in step', 'to toe the line' or 'not to deviate'.

Keeping in step with the Spirit has nothing to do with obeying God in a legalistic way. We aren't under the Mosaic system any more; we belong to Jesus. He died not only to forgive us our sins but to open the door into a new relationship with Him. So we no longer have to go through law to find out how He wants us to live, we go direct to Him.

Jesus speaks to us through His Spirit. He reveals Himself through the Word and puts His desires in our hearts. He calls us to trust Him and to express our gratitude in worship and service. When we don't know what to do, He prompts us, and when we're going wrong, He draws us back into line. Let's live close to Jesus and learn how to keep in step with the Spirit.

➤ In your own words try to define the differences between:

- living by the Spirit
- walking by the Spirit
- being filled with the Spirit.

## ▨ To read

'To walk after the Spirit is to be subject to the Spirit. There is one thing that the man who walks after the Spirit cannot do and that is to be independent of Him. I *must* be subject to the Holy Spirit. The initiative of my life must be with Him. Only as I yield myself to obey Him shall I find the 'the law of the Spirit of life' in full operation and the 'ordinance of law' (all that I have been trying to do to please God) being fulfilled—no longer *by* me but *in* me.'
*Watchman Nee*

He is here. As we open our spirits to the gentle touch of His Spirit, we derive and draw spiritual sustenance from Him. He literally becomes our life. As we allow His Spirit to actually enter our spirits in quiet, still receptivity, He comes in to share life with us (Revelation 3:20).
*W. Phillip Keller*

# No boasting

Let us not become boastful, challenging one another, envying one another (Gal. 5:26 NASB).

O nce Paul has exhorted us to keep in step with the Spirit, he gives us some more examples of the way that the Spirit wants us to live. When we read them, we know that they're true because we're alive to God's desires.

The first attitude that Paul mentions is boasting or conceit. Many of us tend to admire ourselves too much and seek the approval of others. So when we do things we make sure that we're seen in the best possible light and receive much of the glory.

A boastful attitude can prevent people from becoming Christians. They're frightened of what their friends will say if they give their lives to Jesus. Conceit stops us from apologising, confessing a sin or changing our lifestyle. The reason is that we're too embarrassed to humble ourselves and admit the truth.

A well-known psychologist said that people tend to live for self-esteem. His comment mustn't be true of Christians. If our hearts are set on gaining a reputation, we'll damage our relationship with Jesus. Why? Because He'll ask us to do something that looks foolish in the eyes of men — and we'll refuse to do it because we don't want to be ridiculed by others.

## ▓ To memorise

Memorise 1 Corinthians 1:27.

'But God chose the foolish things of the world to shame the wise; God chose the weak things of the world to shame the strong.'

## ▓ To meditate on

Conceit hinders our walk with God. 'How can you believe if you accept praise from one another, yet make no effort to obtain the praise that comes from the only God?' (John 5:44) 'Many even among the leaders believed in him. But because of the Pharisees they would not confess their faith for fear they would be put out of the synagogue; for they loved praise from men more than praise from God' (John 12:42b,43).

Boasting naturally leads to our challenging (provoking) or envying others. When we're proud, we'll provoke someone who challenges our superiority and put on a show of strength just to let him know who's boss.

But if the individual who comes along is more important than we are, we'll envy him. He may have greater authority in the workplace, or be more influential in the church, or simply be more skilful than us. Whatever his qualities, we'll resent them and feel threatened by him.

Jesus was very influential. Crowds listened to Him whenever He preached and His presence unsettled the religious leaders of the day. They didn't want someone around who had greater authority than they had, so they plotted against Him. Even Pilate realised that 'it was out of envy that they had handed Jesus over to him (Matt. 27:18).

If we're keeping step with the Spirit we'll deal with a boastful attitude. We'll also stop provoking those who are weaker than we are and stop envying those who are more able. And we won't be parading ourselves before men. We'll be humbling ourselves and making sure that all the honour and glory go to Jesus.

> ➤ Draw up a personal profile of yourself in a notebook by listing your strong and weak points.

> ➤ Make reference to Romans 12:6–8 and 2 Corinthians 12:9.

## ▨ To challenge

To what extent are you prepared to follow Jesus regardless of what others think?

Are you sure that your answer is more than mere theory? What examples can you give from your own life?

God does not approve of windbags. If there had not been a special need for this warning Paul undoubtedly would not have issued it. Paul's main idea, accordingly, is this: Allow the fruit of the Spirit to expel the works of the flesh!
*William Hendriksen*

# A spirit of gentleness

Brethren, even if a man is caught in any trespass, you who are spiritual, restore such a one in a spirit of gentleness; each one looking to yourself, lest you too be tempted (Gal. 6:1 NASB).

One of the most important aspects of walking in the Spirit concerns the way in which we handle sin in another Christian. Paul says that only a spiritual believer can help someone who's stumbled. In other words, an individual whose life is characterised by the fruit of the Spirit. Now Paul doesn't say that such a person 'can' or 'should try to' restore someone. He implies that if we're walking in the Spirit we should get on with it.

How do we do this? Well, first we must move in the Spirit. Paul has already said that we're not under law and here he implies that a legalistic Christian will never be able to bring someone back from sin. Why? Because he will try to impose rules. 'How disgraceful!' he will say. 'You ought never to have got into that.' His hard moralistic words will have the effect of making someone feel condemned and ashamed. But they won't restore him. The secret lies in a spirit of gentleness, or meekness.

Let's first describe what a gentle spirit isn't. Some people demonstrate a superior attitude when they minister to others. They seem proud of themselves, seek to protect their reputation and gloat over those who fall into sin. They may

## ▓ To identify

Identify three Scriptures which speak about our need to be forgiving.

_____

_____

_____

Is your forgiveness in line with these standards?

## ▓ To meditate on

Paul exhorted and practised gentleness. 'By the meekness and gentleness of Christ, I appeal to you' (2 Cor. 10:1a). 'Be completely humble and gentle; be patient, bearing with one another in love' (Eph. 4:2). 'Let your gentleness be evident to all' (Phil. 4:5a). 'We could have been a burden to you, but we were gentle among you, like a mother caring for her little children' (1 Thess. 2:6b,7).

raise their voices and beat down the individual in an attempt to make him feel guilty.

Certainly God does want people to admit their guilt. It's just that we have no right to make someone feel responsible for sinning against us when he's actually sinned against God. It's the job of the Holy Spirit to convict of sin, not ours. If we pounce judgementally on someone, he will probably be so angry with us that he refuses to listen to us at all.

A spirit of gentleness doesn't come across if you challenge someone's salvation. It's easy to say, 'Since you've committed this sin, you can't possibly be a Christian.' That doesn't help him at all. In fact, he's probably already tormented by the idea that he might not be saved and that God's written him off. He doesn't want further discouragement. He needs reassurance.

Acceptance and forgiveness are at the heart of a spirit of gentleness. The Christian who has sinned needs to feel that you could have done something just as bad as he has — even if it isn't exactly the same sin. We're all weak in different areas, so we must watch that we're not tempted. Let's be sensitive in the way that we deal with those who need restoration.

➤ Think about how you would confront someones's sin in a spirit of gentleness.

➤ Ask a friend to role-play the scene with you.

➤ Afterwards ask them how you came across to them and how they felt as the guilty party.

➤ Revise your approach accordingly.

## ▓ To discern

Do you have a desire to minister to others?

Consider whether this desire is to fulfil your own needs or whether it is truly to help others.

Ask the Lord to help you to discern your own motives.

I am grateful to the Lord who has dusted me off so many times when I have fallen and set me on the path again. If only we had that same love and commitment towards one another instead of treating people harshly in their sin and weakness.
*Floyd McClung*

# Bear one another's burdens

Bear one another's
burdens, and thus fulfill
the law of Christ. For if
anyone thinks he is
something when he is
nothing, he deceives
himself
(Gal. 6:2–3 NASB).

As we've already seen, certain legalists were infiltrating the Galatian church and seeking to encourage the believers to follow the Mosaic law. Here, Paul is telling the Christians, 'Don't put yourself under the law's burden. Instead bear one another's burdens.'

Christ's law is the law of love. You see someone in need of help and you don't ignore him, you take upon yourself the responsibility of carrying his load as though it belonged to you. So if someone falls into sin, you reach out to him and pray with all your heart for his restoration — even if he's your worst enemy. The Mosaic system said nothing of this sort of love. If you're demonstrating it, you'll prove to yourself and others that you're walking in the Spirit. It's one of the greatest tests of legalism.

Some Christians might think that Paul's words, 'if anyone thinks he is something when he is nothing' are too strong, so we must be careful to interpret them in the right way. Clearly Paul doesn't want us to feel totally useless and demoralised. What he's actually saying is that our confidence must not be in ourselves but in God. The stress is on the word 'he'. It means 'he in himself'. So when we seek

## ▓ To list

List four reasons why it is foolish to put our confidence in ourselves rather than in God.

_____

_____

_____

_____

## ▓ To meditate on

We must rely on Christ for everything. 'If a man remains in me and I in him, he will bear much fruit; apart from me you can do nothing' (John 15:5b). 'I am the least of the apostles and do not even deserve to be called an apostle ... But by the grace of God I am what I am, and his grace to me was not without effect. No, I worked harder than all of them — yet not I, but the grace of God that was with me' (1 Cor. 15:9a,10).

to restore another person, we're relying not on our own strength, but on His.

So when you're trying to help someone, how can you be deceived into thinking that you're something when you're nothing? One way is to believe, 'I could never commit that sin.' This is self-righteousness and if you're not careful, you may actually find yourself slipping into sin while you're trying to restore the other person.

Another way of making this mistake is to imagine, I won't be affected by this person's sin. Perhaps he's been overcome in one of the 'deeds of the flesh' that Paul has already mentioned. Let's say it's immorality. Well, you could become so interested in the details of the story that you start being influenced by what the man or woman is saying.

You can also think, 'I'm something' when you've been particularly successful in helping others in the past. Let's say that you have recognised counselling skills. Well, you might assume, 'I'm someone special' simply because of the gift that God has given you.

'Don't be self-deceived,' says Paul. We move on by grace alone. Everything comes from God and all the glory must go to Him.

➤ Read through the story of the Good Samaritan (Luke 10:25–37).

➤ What is the Lord saying to you through this?

➤ Can you equate this story with anything that has happened in your own life?

## ▦ To do

Think about someone you know who is burdened in any way.

Think about what it would mean in practice to bear this burden with them.

Now do it!

Once we understand our real place and purpose in the body of Christ we will then see that we have a responsibility to minister to the needs of others.
*Selwyn Hughes*

# Examine your work

But let each one examine his own work, and then he will have reason for boasting in regard to himself alone, and not in regard to another. For each one shall bear his own load (Gal. 6:4,5 NASB).

There's a progression of thought in Galatians 5:16—6:5. First, Paul talks about resisting the deeds of the flesh, then he speaks about walking by the Spirit. This naturally leads to loving actions towards others and the need for humility. The way to see whether we are humble is to examine ourselves — which is precisely what Paul now encourages us to do.

I think that we instinctively know whether or not we are honouring God. If, for example, someone wrongs us and we say that we've forgiven him, we won't be vindictive towards him and seek to justify our anger. Rather, we'll be reaching out to him in love and praying that God will bless him. A godly reaction will give us an inner assurance that we're doing what's right and that will make us feel good.

Paul has already warned us not to think that we're something when we're nothing. But he doesn't say, 'You mustn't rejoice in your work.' Quite the opposite. He actually encourages us to 'boast' in our service for God when we know that He's blessing it. Such boasting won't come from a proud heart which loudly declares, 'Look at me! Aren't I wonderful?!' It will come from a humble heart which quietly states, 'Look at

## ▓ To examine

Examine *your* work.

If there is anything about your life you would be ashamed of on the day of judgement, deal with it now.

Give thanks to God for all the good things He has worked into your life.

## ▓ To meditate on

There's a right kind of boasting.
'What do you have that you did not receive? And if you did receive it, why do you boast as though you did not?' (1 Cor. 4:7b)
'Let him who boasts boast in the Lord' (2 Cor.10:17).
'Now this is our boast: Our conscience testifies that we have conducted ourselves in the world ... in the holiness and sincerity that are from God' (2 Cor. 1:12).

what God has accomplished through someone like me! Isn't He great?!'

We may think that there's a contradiction between Paul's earlier exhortation to 'bear one another's burdens' and his comment, 'each one shall bear his own load.' But there's no real conflict. In this life we must reach out to others with help and support. But in the last analysis, we're individually responsible to God for the way that we live.

On the day of judgement, we won't be able to say to God, 'I'm sorry I didn't walk more by the Spirit. It was that person's fault actually. He had quite a negative influence on me in that area, so I never did manage to overcome it.' No. On that day, all our excuses will be silenced and each of us will be accountable for what we've done.

Paul tells the Philippians, 'Continue to work our your salvation with fear and trembling, for it is God who works in you to will and to act according to his good purpose' (Phil 2:12b,13). God will work in you by His Spirit, but He won't do everything for you. Make it your aim to please Him so that you won't be ashamed when Jesus returns.

➢ Read Matthew 25:14–30.

➢ Can you equate this parable with your own life?

➢ What have you been given by the master? What are you doing with it?

➢ What do you imagine His response to you will be when He returns?

## ▓ To consider

Give examples of three Bible characters who lived without fear of judgement and three who were aware that they would be judged.

_____  _____

_____  _____

_____  _____

Lord, I am afraid,
I am afraid, for your
   Gospel is terrible.
It is easy to hear it
   preached,
It is relatively easy not to
   be shocked by it,
But it is very difficult to live
   it.
_Michel Quoist_

# Share all good things

Paul's exhortation to 'walk by the Spirit' doesn't stop at the end of Galatians 5. Even in chapter 6 he's outlining what it means to allow the Spirit to rule in our lives.

In verse 6 Paul touches on the subject of church leadership. Now back in chapter 1 of this letter he expressed concern about the preaching of the gospel. 'You mustn't listen to anyone who's distorting the Word,' he told the Galatians. Clearly he wanted the people to hear an unadulterated message — which implied that the leaders had to be careful whenever they proclaimed the truth.

Here, Paul is focusing on the relationship between the teacher and the people who are taught. He wants them to get on well together, so he tells the lay members to 'Share all good things with him who teaches.'

It's commonly understood that Paul is referring to financial provision for those who teach the Word as their full-time occupation. The person in leadership could be a pastor, an elder or a missionary. Whoever they are, we must provide sufficient resources for them.

Having said that, I think that it would be a mistake to confine the meaning of this verse to

## ▨ To do

Find a way of 'sharing good things' with one of your leaders this week.

## ▨ To meditate on

We must honour our leaders.
'The elders who direct the affairs of the church well are worthy of double honour, especially those whose work is preaching and teaching ... "Do not muzzle the ox while it is treading out the grain"' (1 Tim. 5:17,18a).
'Obey your leaders and submit to their authority. They keep watch over you as men who must give an account. Obey them so that their work will be a joy, not a burden' (Heb. 13:17a).

financial support. Paul doesn't say, 'Share your money.' He says, 'Share all good things.' A church leader needs more than a wallet full of banknotes to survive. It's possible for him to feel lonely, isolated and uncared for, and we must ensure that we supply these needs too.

Let's remember that Paul isn't writing to various members of the clergy. He's addressing 'the churches in Galatia' (Gal. 1:2b). He evidently sees it as the responsibility of every believer to take care of those who teach them.

So let me ask you, 'Do you share all good things with those who teach you the Word?' You may be led by a pastor or a team of elders, but do you just assume that they're OK because they're in positions of leadership?

Naturally, it wouldn't be helpful to pry, but maybe there's something more that you could do to support those who teach you. You may feel it appropriate to offer hospitality, or simply to send a card of appreciation or comment favourably on a sermon. Of course, you must check your motives. Some people see this as an opportunity to be 'in' with the leaders. Others genuinely want to serve them more effectively than they have done before.

### ▓ To pray

Pray for your leaders. Pray for their ministry, especially the preaching of the Word. Also pray for them personally, that all their needs will be met — emotional, physical and spiritual.

➢ Paul has already praised the Galations for their treatment of him as a preacher of the gospel (Gal. 4:13).

➢ Find other examples of the responsibilities of the church to those whom God has raised up as leaders.

➢ How does this benefit us all?

High is the honour, precious the privilege, the Creator bestows upon human nature in making man the vehicle to convey Divine truth to his fellow-man. The prophet, the teacher sent from God, echoes the voice which has reached him from above ... This vocation he is bound to fulfil with scrupulous care and unremitting diligence.
*Anon*
*The Expositors Dictionary of Texts*

# How to reap corruption

Do not be deceived,
God is not mocked; for
whatever a man sows,
this he will also reap. For
the one who sows to his
own flesh shall from the
flesh reap corruption
(Gal. 6:7,8a NASB).

When a farmer sows seed, he expects it to produce a crop. That crop doesn't come up immediately. But sooner or later, it's likely to make an appearance.

Paul picks up this farming metaphor and says that we're deceived if we think that we won't reap what we sow. He's speaking not to unbelievers, but to Christians who may be tempted to adopt a casual attitude to their salvation. We can imagine their thinking, 'Now that I'm saved, it doesn't matter how I live.' But Paul turns on this attitude and warns us, as he has done before, not to misuse our freedom.

We may think we're able to get away with things. 'It won't really matter if I get into that,' we say to ourselves. 'It's quite a trivial thing really — hardly a sin as such.' But as we continue to sow to it, we begin to reap from it — and the yield increases the more we sow. Then one day we think, 'It's almost out of control now. I wish I'd stopped right at the beginning.' That's the time when we prove by bitter experience that we can't mock God.

It matters how we live. If we play fast and loose with Him, we'll reap the consequences — 'corruption'. If we allow sin to get a grip on our

## ❊ To illustrate

Illustrate in three examples how we can sow to the flesh and end up reaping sin and its consequences, e.g. overeating resulting in gluttony.

_____

_____

_____

## ❊ To meditate on

Good soil yields a useful crop.
'The seed ... stands for those with a noble and good heart, who hear the word, retain it, and by persevering produce a crop' (Luke 8:15).
'Land that drinks in the rain often falling on it and that produces a crop useful to those for whom it is farmed receives the blessing of God. But land that produces thorns and thistles is worthless and is in danger of being cursed. In the end it will be burned' (Heb. 6:7,8).

life, hell won't snap its jaws at our heels, but corruption will eat into our relationship with God. We won't 'inherit the Kingdom'. We'll lose our sense of God's presence, lack power in our service for Him, and find that our prayers don't get answered. Outwardly we'll go through the Christian motions, but inwardly we'll sense that things aren't right. We'll know that we're growing the wrong crop.

If we sow to the flesh, we won't only reap the consequences on earth, we will also be held accountable in heaven. Paul tells us that 'we must all appear before the judgment seat of Christ, that each one may receive what is due to him for the things done while in the body, whether good or bad' (2 Cor. 5:10). On that day, our work will be tested by fire (1 Cor. 3:10–15). We'll be rewarded for doing good, but penalised if we've persisted in sinful practices.

God doesn't want to rob us of our enjoyment of life. He wants to bless us. That's why He warns us that our conduct will directly affect the amount of blessing that we'll receive. If you want the maximum blessing, you'll sow the maximum obedience and, like the farmer, you'll look forward to reaping in abundance.

### ▨ Food for thought

➤ Read 1 Corinthians 3:10–15. What do you think

- gold, silver and costly stones
- wood, hay and straw

represent?

➤ What are you building with?

### ▨ To answer

Are you being obedient to the Lord?

Review any specific things the Lord has asked you to do.

Are you procrastinating?

Have you done exactly what the Lord asked?

You are in trouble and confusion because you are not honouring God; because you are rebelling against Him; because of your self-will, your arrogance and your pride. You are reaping, says the gospel, what you have sown.
*Martyn Lloyd-Jones*

# How to reap eternal life

... but the one who sows to the Spirit shall from the Spirit reap eternal life (Gal. 6:8b NASB).

The Holy Spirit's role is to hide Himself and glorify Jesus. (John 16:14). Sowing to the Spirit means fitting in with the Spirit's desires. Just as He steps aside and exalts Christ, so we humble ourselves and, like John the Baptist, point others to Jesus.

How do we do this? Through love. By our actions we demonstrate that Jesus is our Lord and that we're living not for ourselves but for Him. We treat others as He would treat them and as we'd like others to treat us. By sowing to the Spirit we produce the fruit of the Spirit — which Paul has already described.

The Bible says, 'Today, if you hear his voice, do not harden your hearts' (Heb. 4:7b). The Spirit speaks to us through the Word or tells us to do things that are in harmony with it. He may ask us to pray or read our Bible more, to give up some sin or to be bolder in our witness. We sow to the Spirit when we listen to His voice and respond to Him.

The result of sowing to the Spirit is that we reap eternal life. Sometimes the phrase 'eternal life' refers to becoming a Christian (John 3:16). Sometimes it speaks about heaven (Mark 10:30). And sometimes, as here, it relates to

## ▓ To read

Read James 5:7,8.

Why is it important to be patient?

_____

_____

_____

## ▓ To meditate on

The Spirit communicates Jesus' desires. 'The Spirit ... will guide you into all truth ... taking what is mine and making it known to you' (John 16:13,14b). 'Those who live in accordance with the Spirit have their minds set on what the Spirit desires' (Rom 8:5b). 'The Spirit searches all things, even the deep things of God ... We have ... received ... the Spirit who is from God, that we may understand what God has freely given us' (1 Cor. 2:10b,12b).

God's blessing on those who are obedient to Him. Paul encouraged Timothy to 'Take hold of the eternal life to which you were called' (1 Tim. 6:12b). And he told the Roman believers, 'If by the Spirit you put to death the misdeeds of the body, you will live' (Rom. 8:13b). In other words, you'll experience Life with a capital 'L'.

Paul says, 'Godliness has value for all things, holding promise for both the present life and the life to come' (1 Tim. 4:8b). Every believer has the certainty of eternal life, but not all of them are practising godliness here on earth.

If we want to enjoy God's blessing both now and in heaven, we will sow to the Spirit and reap the fulness of eternal life. As we do this, we will enjoy the favour of God. He will draw close to us and speak to us through His Word. He will answer our prayers and release His power in us. We'll be conscious of His intimate presence and also of His hand of blessing on everything that we do.

Jesus always intended us to have life 'to the full' (John 10:10b). Since we'll reap in exact proportion to the way in which we sow, we effectively decide for ourselves how 'full' our life will be.

➢ Read 1 Timothy 2:1,2; 3:16; 4:7; 6:6,11.

➢ What do you glean about godliness from these verses in Paul's letter to Timothy?

## ■ To respond

How do you feel you should respond to this teaching on sowing and reaping?

_____

_____

_____

(the attention of) the godly person ... is focused on Christ's objective for him, and his eye is fixed on heaven. He is God-centred in his devotion, and he strives to be Godlike in his character.
*Jerry Bridges*

# Don't grow weary

And let us not lose heart in doing good, for in due time we shall reap if we do not grow weary (Gal. 6:9 NASB).

W hen someone first believes in Christ, weariness usually isn't a problem. The recent convert explores his new faith with obvious enthusiasm and laps up every blessing that comes in his direction.

But as time passes, he begins to realise that the Christian life isn't as straightforward as he first thought. He starts to face difficulties. Maybe things happen that seem to suggest that God has abandoned him. He has to endure severe persecution at home or at work, he goes through a time of personal suffering and is tempted to become discouraged because God doesn't appear to be answering his prayers.

It isn't long before he discovers that the Lord wants to deal with his character and is pointing out various sinful practices which badly need attention. The world, the flesh and the devil seem to conspire against him. He does his best to live uprightly, but the battles are often fierce and the blessings delayed.

Many of us have experienced his frustration. We do all that we can to live righteously and confidently assert, 'I believe that I'll reap what I sow.' But time passes and we don't seem to be reaping much. 'Maybe I should try harder to

## ▒ To define

What is the distinction between weariness and genuine tiredness?

_____

_____

_____

## ▒ To meditate on

We must keep going.
'And as for you, brothers, never tire of doing what is right' (2 Thess. 3:13).
'Consider him who endured such opposition from sinful men, so that you will not grow weary and lose heart' (Heb. 12:3).
'You have persevered and have endured hardships for my name, and have not grown weary' (Rev. 2:3).

please God,' we think. Then we fall into legalism which turns a once-joyful experience of Jesus into a wearisome trail of good works.

Sometimes our weariness is the result of pride. We start something thinking, 'I'm sure I can do this,' but we're trusting in ourselves. For a while things seem to go well, but then we run out of strength and become lethargic. In this case, we must confess our sin of self-confidence and turn to God for His enabling.

But it's hard when we seek to glorify God and there seems to be no response from Him. 'I can't understand it,' we think. 'Where's the blessing? Has He noticed what I'm doing or am I working in a vacuum?' As time passes we're likely to conclude, 'Sowing and reaping might work for other people, but evidently not for me.'

Paul anticipates this reaction. He knows that 'doing good' involves a lot of effort and that the apparent absence of blessing could easily result in our giving up. So he warns us not to let this happen. 'In due time we shall reap,' he says. It's a statement of fact, a certainty — but there's a condition attached to it. If you want to reap, don't grow weary. Keep sowing to the Spirit and God will reward you when the time is right.

> Study Isaiah 40:27–31.

> What is the key to drawing on God's infinite strength and power?

## ▨ To acknowledge

What things in your own life might tempt you to grow weary and give up?

_____

_____

Confess them to God and let Him refresh and envision you.

**If you're tired, go to bed.
If you're weary, go to God!**
_David Holden_
_Downs Bible Week_

# How to avoid weariness

And let us not lose heart in doing good, for in due time we shall reap if we do not grow weary. So then, while we have opportunity, let us do good to all men, and especially to those who are of the household of the faith (Gal. 6:9,10 NASB).

There are a number of ways in which we can avoid weariness in the Christian life. Let's highlight some of them.

Firstly, we must make sure that we're in the will of God, doing the 'good' that He wants us to do. If we're not sure whether He's called us to a certain work, we'll come unstuck when we hit problems because we won't have the faith that He'll see us through. Then our uncertainty will result in weariness and indecision.

But if we've sought God concerning His will for our lives and if we're obeying Him, then we'll be confident no matter what happens. When things begin to get difficult, we'll simply remind ourselves, God has called me to this. I'm doing the good works that He 'prepared in advance for [me] to do' (Eph. 2:10). I know that He will help me to overcome in His strength.

Secondly, we must remember the principle of the time gap. When Paul says that we'll reap in 'due time', he's using an illustration from agriculture. If a farmer sows seed, he doesn't expect it to come up the next day. It has to mature in the earth before it produces a yield.

A spiritual harvest rarely comes immediately but it will come. Paul says that we *shall* reap.

## ▓ To do

Find a way of 'doing good' to a fellow Christian during the coming week.

## ▓ To meditate on

We will all receive our 'just deserts'. 'Surely you will reward each person according to what he has done' (Ps. 62:12b).
'The wicked man earns deceptive wages, but he who sows righteousness reaps a sure reward' (Prov. 11:18).
'He who sows wickedness reaps trouble' (Prov. 22:8a).
'Peacemakers who sow in peace raise a harvest of righteousness' (James 3:18).

It's impossible to pursue a godly or a godless lifestyle without reaping the consequences.

Thirdly, we must neither be too lazy nor too busy. If we're lazy, we'll expect God to do everything for us. If we're over-busy, we'll try to do everything for God. Both extremes are likely to hinder our relationship with Him. On the one hand, we won't be bothered to spend time in His presence; on the other, we won't have time to do so. God usually reveals Himself through the Word and prayer. We must fiercely guard our times of fellowship with Him.

Finally, we must keep our eyes on Jesus. Christians often exhaust themselves because they're struggling to please people. But it was never God's intention to weary us. Jesus' yoke is easy and His burden is light. If we live solely for Him, we'll discover the truth of these words.

Paul sums up this section by encouraging us again to 'do good' — both to all people and also to fellow Christians. We must be careful not to lose touch with unbelievers when God wants us to serve them. We must also be aware of needs of individuals and groups within the church and be prepared to reach out to them in any way that we can.

## ▨ To evaluate

lazy                                    over-busy
|_____|

On the line above mark where you would place yourself between these two extremes.

What steps could you take to achieve the right balance?

> ➤ Spend time reading and meditating on Psalm 62.

My friend, if you think of your Christian life in any shape or form with this sense of grudge, or as a wearisome task or duty ... Look at the world in its evil and sin, look at the hell to which it was leading you, and then look forward and realize that you are set in the midst of the most glorious campaign into which a man could ever enter, and that you are on the noblest road that the world has ever known.
*Martyn Lloyd-Jones*

# Boasting in the flesh

See with what large letters I am writing to you with my own hand. Those who desire to make a good showing in the flesh try to compel you to be circumcised, simply that they may not be persecuted for the cross of Christ. For those who are circumcised do not even keep the Law themselves, but they desire to have you circumcised, that they may boast in your flesh (Gal. 6:11–13 NASB).

In the ancient world it was customary for authors to dictate their letters to someone who would write down what they said. Paul used a scribe (Rom. 16:22), but it seems that he adopted the habit of adding the last few words in his own handwriting — as we can see from his epistle to the Galatians.

One of his reasons for doing this was to establish the genuineness of his letters. He had many enemies, some of whom could easily have circulated material claiming, 'This is from Paul.' By writing the concluding remarks in his letters himself, Paul ensured that his readers would know that he was the author.

In some cultures, if you want to emphasise something you've written, you might underline or capitalise it. In ancient days, you wrote it in 'large letters'. Paul did this in his epistle to the Galatians because he was keen to stress something that he'd been saying. As he signed off, he wanted his readers to have ringing in their ears the most important point of his message: 'Don't put yourselves under the Law.'

The reason why the legalists in Galatia were returning to the Law of Moses was this: they wanted to avoid persecution. They wanted to

## ▓ To discover

Read Ephesians 4:14–16 and Colossians 2:8.

How can Christians learn to recognise the truth?

_____

_____

## ▓ To meditate on

Let's not be deceived.
'I urge you, brothers, to watch out for those who cause divisions and put obstacles in your way that are contrary to the teaching you have learned. Keep away from them. For such people are not serving our Lord Christ, but their own appetites. By smooth talk and flattery they deceive the minds of naïve people' (Rom. 16:17,18).

circumcise the Christians so they could boast in their flesh. They were advocating the sort of religion that unbelievers love to embrace.

The biblical message of salvation by grace is intensely irritating to the natural man. If you tell someone that he's a sinner who stands under the judgement of God and that there's nothing he can do to save himself, his reaction will probably be, 'How dare you suggest such terrible things? I'm as good as the next man — doing my best. You're way out of line.'

When you see that he's beginning to get angry, you might be tempted to say, 'Well, er, the situation really isn't that bad. You could do a few things to help yourself — like love others more.' By responding this way, you've avoided persecution by appealing to a legalistic gospel. You've flattered him into thinking that he can do something to contribute to his salvation. You're boasting in his flesh.

The legalists in Galatia were inconsistent. They wanted to put the believers under the Law which they themselves didn't keep. We cannot fulfil God's holy requirements. If we try to add our righteousness to Jesus' perfect sacrifice, we will lose all assurance of our salvation.

➢ Read Matthew 10:17–23; 2 Timothy 3:12.

➢ How can persecution be seen as something positive?

## ▨ To assess

Have you ever been tempted to water down the gospel message when witnessing?

In retrospect what could you have said or done differently?

So the vital question for us is not what is going to happen to the world as such, but what is going to happen to me; what of my soul? That is the emphasis and that has generally been a cause of offence to men and women, this narrowness of the gospel, in that it limits its interests to this one question.
*Martyn Lloyd-Jones*

# Boasting in the cross

But may it never be
that I should boast,
except in the cross of
our Lord Jesus Christ,
through which the
world has been
crucified to me, and I
to the world. For neither
is circumcision
anything, nor
uncircumcision, but a
new creation. And
those who will walk by
this rule, peace and
mercy be upon them,
and upon the Israel of
God. From now on let
no one cause trouble
for me, for I bear on my
body the brand-marks
of Jesus. The grace of
our Lord Jesus Christ be
with your spirit,
brethren. Amen
(Gal. 6:14–18 NASB).

While the legalists in Galatia were focusing people's attention on how they could keep the Mosaic Law, Paul's eyes were fixed on the cross. Once he had been preoccupied with trying to please God by keeping rules. Now he was trusting in Christ alone.

Before Paul became a Christian, he was interested in the world. He was Gamaliel's star pupil and was headed for a promising career in law. But immediately he was saved, the world lost interest in him — because he no longer belonged to its system, and he likewise lost interest in the world — because it rejected Christ. The two were crucified to each other.

Worldly ways of pleasing God are irrelevant for Christians because we've died to them. Circumcision and uncircumcision are alike unimportant. Self-imposed rules do nothing to change us. What matters is that we're a new creation on the inside. When we know that Christ's sacrifice satisfies the Father on our behalf, we'll stop struggling to succeed and boast only in the cross.

At this point in his letter, Paul plays on words. Up to now, he's been telling his readers not to follow rules; now he mentions the 'rule'

## ▓ To assess

What preoccupies you most? (Be honest.)

_____

_____

## ▓ To meditate on

Christians don't belong to the world.
'I have given them your word and the world has hated them, for they are not of the world any more than I am of the world' (John 17:14).
'Anyone who chooses to be a friend of the world becomes an enemy of God' (James 4:4b).
'The reason the world does not know us is that it did not know him' (1 John 3:1b).

that's worth following. The Law of Moses never brought 'peace and mercy'. Quite the opposite: it actually disturbed people's sense of peace and condemned them without mercy. It will always do this if we try to live by it.

It's as if Paul is saying, 'Since you Galatians are so keen to pursue some sort of law, here's a rule for you: trust Jesus and respond to the Spirit. If you really want to be a true child of Abraham and an heir to all the promises, you won't put yourselves under Law. Instead, you'll realise that Abraham wasn't justified by any law at all, but by faith. The true "Israel of God" receive peace and mercy only when they glory in the cross of Christ.'

At the end of his letter, Paul appeals to the Galatians to stop troubling him over the matter of the Law because he has nothing further to say about it. The scars on his body reveal the extent of his persecution for the sake of the gospel, and it remains only for the Galatians to respond to what he's said. 'Reject this legalism once and for all,' he effectively declares. 'It's robbed you of all your joy. Christ is sufficient. Trust only in Him and the blessing will come flooding back to you.'

➤ Review all the previous studies.

➤ Complete any unfinished assignments.

➤ Write down in a notebook the main things you have learned and how you have changed as a result of working through these studies.

➤ Set yourself helpful goals which will help you put into practice all that you've learned.

## ▓ To reflect

'For we maintain that a man is justified by faith apart from observing the law' (Rom. 3:28).

Paul restates this theme again and again in his letters.

Have you got the message?

If you are still battling with legalism in your life, you may find it helpful to get your pastor to pray for you.

Forbid it, Lord, that I should boast
Save in the cross of Christ my God.
All the vain things that charm me most,
I sacrifice them to His blood.
Isaac Watts
'When I Survey The Wondrous Cross'

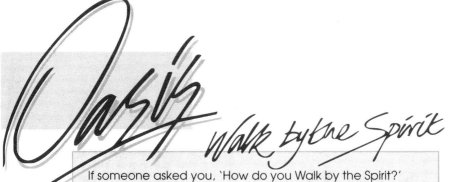

## Walk by the Spirit

If someone asked you, 'How do you Walk by the Spirit?' what answer would you give? Michael Eaton takes you systematically through Galatians chapters 5 and 6 and provides clear teaching on the way that God wants you to live.

He points out that the Galatian Christians were losing the joy of their salvation because they were trying to put themselves under the Mosaic Law. Then he helps you to recognise and overcome legalism in your own life. He introduces the law of love and explains how you can resist temptation and develop the fruit of the Spirit. There are also exercises to help you work out in practice what you're learning on paper. The exercises will involve you in meditation and memorisation of Scripture, writing down your own opinions, and practical assignments.

Oasis notes are structured to provide sufficient material so that you take two days to cover each study, and therefore two months to complete the book. If you take your time, you are more likely to benefit; and the important thing is not that you finish fast, but that you hear from God!

Michael Eaton grew up in London, but now lives in Kenya. He is one of the leaders of the Chrisco Fellowship, Nairobi, which draws about 2,000 people to its prayer meetings.

WORD
BOOKS

WORD BOOKS
Nelson Word Ltd
Milton Keynes, England
£1.99
Catalogue Number YB 9807

ISBN 0-85009-807-6

00199

9 780850 098075